THE BASIC GOURMET

THE BASIC GOURMET

100 Foolproof Recipes and Essential Techniques for the Beginning Cook

by
Diane Morgan,
Dan Taggart, Kathleen Taggart, and
Georgia Vareldzis

Photographs by

Pavlina Eccless

Chronicle Books • San Francisco

Library of Congress Cataloging-in-Publication Data available.

Design: Nancy E. Koc
Food Stylist: George Dolese
Set in Monotype Joanna Roman and Italic and Gill Sans

Our thanks to the following stores for their generous lending of photography props:
Collections, Country Lane Traditional Furniture, Crate and Barrel, Fillamento, Mac,
Pottery Barn, The Gardener.

Printed in Hong Kong.

ISBN 0-8118-0476-3

Distributed in Canada by
Raincoast Books
112 East Third Ave.
Vancouver, B.C. V5T 1C8

10 9 8 7 6 5 4 3 2 1

CHRONICLE BOOKS
275 FIFTH STREET
SAN FRANCISCO, CA 94103

Contents

Acknowledgments

We are very grateful for the support and encouragement we have received for this project. Elise Goodman believed in the project from the start and worked many hours to help us put together and deliver a competent proposal. We are also grateful to our competent and responsive editor, Jacqueline Killeen, as well as senior editor Bill LeBlond. Barb Durbin has been a great hometown booster for all our books, and it was her idea for the Kitchen Klutz class that helped get this book going. We also appreciate all the students in the Kitchen Klutz classes for helping us focus on their beginning cooking needs.

No cookbook is worth its salt unless the recipes have been well tested, and we've had some great testers. Betty Shenberger has long been our favorite tester, booster, and food idea person. Our other guinea pigs (uh, testers) include Laurie Briggs, Jane Burkholder, Vicki DeVito, Craig Fuller, Ed Gowans, Geri Haber, Tom and Sue Horstmann, Cheryl Jackson, Jim and Vicki Jakovec, Dan Koch, Jodi McClain, and last but not least, Greg Morgan. Thanks all!

INTRODUCTION

This book is all about you having fun in the kitchen.

We are four authors who would rather cook than do practically anything else in the world. You, on the other hand, may not know a chef's knife from a potato masher. We long to sauté, to poach, to grill, to roast. You may wonder why an oven needs to be preheated, or why grilling with the lid on makes food taste better, or what the difference is between a saucepan and a stockpot.

Learning to cook is a lot like learning to ride a bicycle. Early attempts are often disastrous. Since kitchens don't come with training wheels, lots of people skin their knees in the process of trying to produce their first real meals—the ones that don't come frozen in a carton listing oven or microwave instructions. New cooks, young or old, just need to master a few techniques—like a bicycle rider—to make life in the kitchen easier and more rewarding.

We know what it feels like to be a new cook. We've used stopwatches trying to follow stir-frying instructions; we've added coffee grounds to recipes calling for "coffee"; we've added salt before tasting a soup made with canned broth; we've beaten our cake batters for minutes to make certain everything is well mixed. We've laughed and cried at the same time over our own private food disasters!

This book is intended to make you comfortable in the kitchen. We offer tips on kitchen equipment, basic cooking terminology, cooking methods and timing, and recipe variations. We call for ingredients that make a difference in flavor but are available in most American supermarkets. The foods in this book are mostly modern-day "basic American," even if their ethnic roots go back to other places and times.

Great cooking is often simple cooking. Imagine a rich, nutty chocolate brownie, served warm from the pan without any adornment at all; a plate of mixed lettuces, tossed with just good olive oil, not too much fine vinegar, salt, and freshly ground pepper; or a crusty hamburger patty, hot off the grill, oozing rivulets of pink juices, served with fresh, chewy bread. These are world-class dishes easily within the capability of beginning cooks.

So smile, gentle reader, and follow us into the kitchen. We're going to teach you how to boil an egg without burning the water!

KITCHEN BASICS

A solid foundation for the beginning cook—equipment, ingredients, terms, and techniques

STARTING A KITCHEN

Life isn't fair to most beginning cooks. Just as the interest in good cooking (or at least good eating) begins to develop, some recipe writer demands the use of a piece of equipment probably not found even in the *White House* commissary! The truth is that good tools make kitchen work easier, just as they do in other endeavors, but the President's sautéed chicken doesn't taste any better coming out of a copper sauté pan than yours will taste cooked in a stainless steel skillet. If you buy a few quality tools for your kitchen before you spend all your money on fancy serving pieces, you'll have more fun cooking and get better results. The following is a suggested cooking arsenal designed to help you get the job done in the kitchen with the least frustration.

Cookware

For a beginning cook it must be overwhelming to walk into a cookware store and try to decide what saucepan or frying pan to buy, let alone a set of cookware. It is no different an experience than when any of us walks into a stereo store and tries to make choices when our knowledge base is limited. We want an "expert" just to give us the answer. Let us try to be the "experts" here and guide you through some of the options.

Here is our suggested list of cookware that will cover most kitchen requirements:

1½- to 2-quart saucepan with lid
3½- to 4-quart saucepan with lid
8- to 10-quart stockpot with lid
8- and 12-inch frying pans
10-inch nonstick frying pan
3- and 6-quart straight-sided frying pans with lids
   (Dutch sauté pans)
Broiler/roasting pan

First, go through your kitchen and figure out if any of your equipment matches our list. A 2½ quart saucepan is a close match to our 1½- to 2-quart saucepan. Decide if it is in good shape. If it burns everything you put into it because it is so thin and lightweight, it probably is ready to be replaced. Cookware, however, is expensive—cookware that lasts, that is—so replace your pans as your budget allows. It is better to have fewer pans of good quality than a whole brand-new set that won't hold up over time.

Now comes the question "What is the best cookware?" There is no honest answer to that question, but we do have opinions! None of us has a "complete set" of any particular brand of cookware, primarily because different materials are better for different cooking tasks. For instance, it is wonderful to have a nonstick frying pan for scrambling eggs, but we certainly would not want a saucepan that is used with a wire whisk to be made of a nonstick material. Over time that saucepan will be scratched from the whisk. It would be preferable to have a saucepan lined with stainless steel or made from anodized aluminum. So, let's get specific and discuss these pans one by one.

Saucepans. The 1½- to 2-quart saucepan with lid is the right size for cooking rice or small amounts of vegetables and warming small quantities of food, such as soups. The larger 3½- to 4-quart saucepan with lid is used for cooking small amounts of pasta, boiling vegetables, making pudding, and heating soups. We prefer All-Clad, Chantal SL, and Cuisinart Commercial cookware in these sizes because they cook evenly, with no hot spots.

Stockpot. For cooking large batches of soup, stew, chili, and spaghetti sauce you will need an 8- to 10-quart stockpot with lid. If you are only going to cook pasta in this size pot, an inexpensive aluminum pan will work well. (Untreated aluminum will react with acid foods such as tomatoes, so avoid it if you plan to use the pot for multiple purposes.) Our preference for an all-purpose pot in this size range would be All-Clad or Cuisinart Commercial, because quality will be your ally. Le Creuset also makes great cookware in this category, but we caution you that they are heavy.

Frying pans. A well-seasoned cast iron 8- to 12-inch frying pan is great for frying fish or potatoes, sautéing meat, and frying chicken. It is our favorite for these tasks because the food browns so well. A 10-inch nonstick frying pan is perfect for scrambled or fried eggs, or any low-fat frying. You can buy an inexpensive one, but don't expect it to last too long. Some brands we recommend are All-Clad, Calphalon, Meyer (heavyweight only), Scanpan, and T-Fal.

Large straight-sided frying pans. A good all-around pot for braising meat, cooking pot roast, roasting chicken (use the larger size pan), and cooking vegetables is a 3- or 6-quart straight-sided frying pan, preferably with ovenproof handles. Among the brands we like are All-Clad, Chantal SL, and Cuisinart Commercial.

Broiler/roasting pan. These are usually about 2 inches deep and made of stainless steel or aluminum, sometimes in a nonstick finish. Some have a slotted cover, which serves as a broiler rack, or a heavy wire rack, which fits inside the pan.

While we have mentioned some specific brand names in the preceding discussion, you may not have a clue what they look like, nor what would differentiate them. To help you make some educated buying decisions, here are a few additional comments. Three of the brands mentioned above (All-Clad, Cuisinart Commercial, and Chantal SL) are made of durable stainless steel and feature added layers of copper or aluminum on the bottom (and all the way up the sides in the case of All-Clad), which spread the heat evenly. This layering of metals is referred to as "sandwiching." Copper and aluminum are great conductors of heat, making them ideal materials to sandwich between an outer and inner layer of stainless steel. Stainless steel on the inside of a pan is perfect because it is totally nonreactive to foods. For the outside of a pan, stainless is desirable because of its beauty, low maintenance, and durability. Copper is beautiful, too, but be prepared to do some polishing.

Good cookware costs money. Pay it. Nothing is as frustrating in the midst of preparing a meal as watching food burn in the bottom of lightweight, inexpensive pans. The heavier construction of better quality cookware will make your life in the kitchen easier for many years. Cheap cookware wastes expensive food. You can expect to pay approximately $200 to $400 for a 5- to 9-piece set of the brands mentioned. Individual pans range from about $70 to $95 for a 1½ quart saucepan to about $150 to $180 for a 6-quart straight-sided frying pan. You may be able to find better deals during sales.

Cutlery

We recommend what is usually called "high carbon stainless" knives for the kitchen. They don't rust under normal circumstances or discolor when used on acid foods. High carbon stainless is a little softer than old-fashioned stainless, so you can keep your knives sharp by using a sharpening "steel." Ask for a lesson in using the sharpening steel when you buy your knives. A dull knife takes more time and effort to use; despite that, sharp knives seem to be as rare as hens' teeth in American kitchens.

A good basic knife collection would include the following at least:
8- or 10-inch chef's knife
Serrated bread knife
3- or 4-inch paring knife
Sharpening steel

A number of good brands of knives is available. Some have wooden handles, others have handles made of more exotic materials, such as polypropylene. What you choose for the handle in large part will be determined by how the knife feels in your hand. When you are buying knives, hold the different handles, see what feels comfortable; some brands seem to have a better fit for small hands. The construction of the knife is a big factor in determining its quality. Some knives have one-piece construction from tip of blade to end of handle ("full-tang"), others don't. Full-tang knives usually have better balance and will last longer in return for a slightly higher investment. Some quality brands to shop for are: Dexter (Russell Harrington), Henckels, Gerber, Marks, Wusthöf-Trident, Forschner, Chicago Cutlery. Other regional or small manufacturers may have something to offer in your area; just ask for an explanation of quality. (But be sure to avoid the "Guaranteed sharp for thirty years!" kind of cheap, lightweight goods usually shown slicing through logs, cardboard, or tin cans on late-night television!)

Good knives are an investment, and a worthwhile one at that. If well taken care of, they should last a lifetime. You can expect to pay about $125 total for the three knives plus sharpening steel listed above, from a brand such as Gerber. Top-of-the-line knives, such as Henckels Four Star series, will cost approximately $175 total for the same three knives and sharpening steel. Again, buy according to your budget; any of the brands mentioned will work well.

Thermometers

Instant-read thermometer. A small-dial, thin-shaft, all-purpose tool used for measuring the temperature of everything from roast chicken to grilled fish to cooked custard. Most read from about 60°F to 220°F, give a reading within a few seconds (hence the "instant-read" nomenclature), and make a very small hole in meat, poultry, or fish. These thermometers are not made to leave in the oven—the dials are usually plastic and would melt. Better models have a nut on the back of the dial to allow recalibration in the event the instrument is dropped or banged around. This invaluable tool is the hands-down best way to know when something is cooked to the required temperature. Quality brands include Northwest Component Design's Insta-Read, Cuisinart, Taylor, and Tel-True.

Oven thermometer. Helps you find out how far off your oven's thermostat may be, so that you can adjust the temperature dial accordingly. Place on a middle rack, and check 15 to 20 minutes after the oven has been set to the desired temperature. Some models have a dial with a red pointer (probably the least accurate), others, called "spirit-stem," have a glass tube in which red fluid goes up and down. These are the most common and will get the job done. Digital models are now being made. These are the easiest to read, but likely more expensive. If cost is a factor, stick with the spirit-stem type. Brand names include the same as listed for instant-read thermometers.

Cutting Boards

Polypropylene cutting board. About 9x15 inches. These are easy on knives and go into a dishwasher for cleaning and sanitizing—an especially important factor because salmonella bacteria are usually present in raw poultry and other raw meats; washing in the dishwasher helps kill the bacteria. They are inexpensive enough to allow you to buy two, so you'll have one to use while the other is in the dishwasher. We like the relatively nontextured variety,

finding that more surface nibs or pattern make it more difficult to achieve clean slices.

Wooden carving board. Buy one with a "moat" and "well." For carving chicken, roasts, etc. at the table or in the kitchen. The moat collects the juices while the well traps them, avoiding major messes when carving cooked meats. If you can afford it, buy one larger than the poly board.

Measuring Tools

Measuring spoons. A set of stainless steel measuring spoons (better yet, two sets). Won't corrode in the dishwasher or while sitting in salad dressing or other acidic foods.

Dry measuring cups. A set of stainless steel measuring cups, ¼ cup to 1 cup. Designed to be filled to slightly over-flowing, then leveled off to give exact measure. For dry measure of flour, crumbs, sugar, etc. Plastic works but gets thrown around in the dishwasher a lot more.

Liquid measuring cups. Glass or clear plastic. We suggest having three sizes: 1-, 2-, and 4-cup measures. Designed with see-through markings and pour spouts.

Mixing Bowls

A set of mixing bowls, in four sizes: about 2-quart, 3-quart, 4-quart, and 6-quart. Available in stainless steel, heatproof glass, ceramic, and soft or hard plastic. Brands include Pyrex, Rosti, Copco, Bia-Cordon Bleu, and many more. Stainless

will last the longest, but colorful melamine (plastic) pleases the eyes and is quieter while stirring. You decide. When in doubt, buy a larger size; you can always do a small job in a large bowl, but not the other way around.

Other Utensils

Baking pan. A 9x13-inch glass or metal baking pan with sides 1 to 2 inches high is useful for cakes, brownies, roasting meats, etc.

Baking (cookie) sheet with sides/jelly roll pan. Generally made of aluminum or stainless steel, they are also available with nonstick coating. Dimensions vary, but 10x15 and 12x18 inches are pretty common sizes. Sides of 3/4 inch or more allow batters to be poured into the pan, such as for layer cakes or brownies. This pan can also be used as a broiler/roasting pan when fitted with a rack.

Cake tester. A thin wire with a handle used to insert into cakes, batter breads, etc. to check doneness. A toothpick will work in a pinch.

Colander. Available in plastic or metal for draining noodles, fruits, vegetables, etc. We prefer stainless steel since it dries better in a dishwasher, doesn't corrode, and won't melt if accidentally set on a range top.

Cooling rack. A flat, wire rack used to cool breads, cakes, cookies, etc.

Flexible rubber spatulas. Buy both large and small sizes. Any decent kitchen store—or even your supermarket—has several choices. These are indispensable for scraping the last scrap of food from measuring cups and bowls and for certain mixing jobs. Rubbermaid, Rosti, Dr. Oetker are among quality brands.

Fresh pepper grinder. For us, freshly ground pepper is a must, so a grinder is a "must have" for the kitchen. They come in wood, plastic, and steel. Buy according to your taste and decor, but we prefer a grinder mechanism that allows for variable coarseness of grind. Having a utilitarian one for the kitchen and a nice one for the table is a luxury, but something to keep in mind when making your purchase. A company called Olde Thompson makes great wooden pepper grinders, and the good quality steel ones are made in France by Perfect.

Garlic press. A metal or plastic tool that squeezes a clove of garlic through small perforations.

Grater. A stainless steel four-sided grater gives a choice of grating coarseness and won't rust.

Gravy strainer (fat separator). This looks like a measuring cup with a spout that pours liquid only from the bottom of the cup. Since fat rises to the top of liquids, the juice that is poured is mostly fat free. Some models have a spring-loaded opening at the bottom instead of a spout. These are most often made of clear, heatproof plastic, but glass models have been on the market, too.

Juice squeezers. A fluted, cone-shaped tool used to extract the juice of citrus fruits. Can be manual or electric.

Mortar and pestle. A marble, wood, or ceramic bowl along with a bulb-shaped pounder used for crushing herbs, spices, and seeds into powders and pastes.

Muffin pan. A 12-cup version is widely available in every material from plain aluminum to nonstick coated steel or aluminum.

Pastry brush. One with natural bristles about 2 inches wide is a very handy size. Long-lasting ones have wooden handles and look a little like a paint brush.

Roasting rack. You are probably familiar with the flat ones, but an adjustable, V-shaped roasting rack is your best choice.

Salad spinner. Available in lots of colors and styles, this plastic gadget is the easiest way to dry greens for salads so that the dressing stays on the greens. We used to laugh. Then we used one. We don't laugh anymore.

Sifter. For lightening flour mixtures and mixing in leavenings and seasonings. They are made of tinned steel or stainless steel. Tinned steel may rust eventually, but may cost less initially.

Slotted spoons. A large spoon with holes. Used to remove solid foods from cooking liquids.

Stainless steel wire whisks. Used for mixing sauces, salad dressings, etc., they won't rust. We suggest an 8-inch and a 12-inch whisk. "Best" is among brands known for quality.

Strainers. A bowl-shaped, metal mesh device used to

separate solid foods from cooking liquids. Comes in various sizes. We recommend those with a handle.

Tongs. About 9 to 10 inches long, preferably spring-action and made of stainless steel.

Vegetable peeler. The swivel-action, metal-handle variety is available in left- and right-handed models. Buy the sharpest one you can find. In our experience the carbon steel (not stainless) blade looks rusty after use but is sharper and therefore easier to use.

Wok. An optional piece of equipment, but ideal for stir-frying. We prefer woks 12 to 14 inches in diameter and made of heavy-gauge steel, which needs to be seasoned. Woks that are used right on a cooktop are preferable to those that have their own plug-in heating unit.

Wooden spoons. Buy several sizes and shapes, perhaps 8 to 14 inches in length. They don't melt, won't scratch cookware, are quiet to use, are inexpensive, and survive a dishwasher better than most people think. Various woods are used; beechwood and olive wood seem especially long-lasting to us.

Zester. A hand-held gadget that removes the zest (colored part of the rind without the white pith underneath) of an orange, grapefruit, lemon, or lime when drawn across the skin of the fruit.

Larger Equipment

If the money is there, we would suggest the following items.

Blender. This is not a place to spend a lot of money considering that a quality food processor is a more versatile kitchen tool. However, for puréeing soups, nothing works better. Look for one on sale at your local discount store.

Food processor. We suggest you buy a quality machine or forget the whole idea. Our experience is that Cuisinart makes the broadest range of sizes and is usually the most powerful in its class. One fast way to judge competitors of equal capacity is to pick up each machine. The one that weighs the most is likely the most powerful. Buy the largest machine you can afford. Larger machines chop more uniformly and perform better when handling heavier tasks such as making bread dough or cookies.

Microwave oven. Fast becoming a universal kitchen appliance. We use one all the time, particularly as a tool for melting and reheating. We suggest you look for the following features: largest size you can fit in your kitchen and afford; electronic controls—seconds count in microwave cookery; 650 or 700 watts of power; removable or recessed turntable if there is one; 5 to 10 power settings—you don't need more.

Stand or hand-held mixer. A stand mixer is built into a large metal or plastic housing onto which its bowl is placed. Just turn on the machine and watch the mixing take place. KitchenAid is the most universally available premium brand; lots of cooks like the British import, Kenwood. Other domestic brands may be available in your area. Small, portable hand-held mixers are fine for light-duty jobs like whipping cream; cookie dough requires one of the heavy-duty brands, such as Krups.

A GUIDE TO INGREDIENTS

The following ingredients, unless otherwise noted, are commonly found in well-stocked grocery stores and supermarkets.

Baking powder. A white powder used as a leavening agent in baked goods to make them rise. Always buy double-acting baking powder; this compound is heat-activated.

Baking soda. A white powder used as a leavening agent in baked goods to make them rise. This compound is used in recipes that include acidic ingredients, such as buttermilk, lemon juice, vinegar, etc. Baking soda is activated by the acid in the recipe. Frequently recipes use both baking powder and baking soda.

Butter. Our preference is for unsalted butter. We have found that it allows the cook to control the salt content and is often a fresher product. If you substitute salted butter, use less salt in the recipe.

Capers. The pickled buds of a plant found in the Mediterranean. Size varies greatly; generally the larger capers are more expensive. After opening, store in the refrigerator; they keep indefinitely.

Chocolate. Two types of baking chocolate are used in this book, unsweetened (without added sugar) and semisweet. Both are sold in solidified blocks or chips, as opposed to cocoa, the powdered form. If you develop an interest in baking, you will find great quality differences in semisweet chocolates. Brands found in your typical grocery store are fine, but specialty stores will carry brands such as Callebaut, Lindt, Tobler, and Guittard. Taste and discover your own preferences.

Cilantro (fresh coriander). A fresh herb used in Mexican, Asian, and East Indian cooking. It has a wonderful taste to some, and to others it tastes like soap. You decide.

Cocoa. Dried, ground, or powdered chocolate. It is available either sweetened (for chocolate drinks) or unsweetened (for use in baking).

Coffee. In this book, for baking purposes we use instant coffee granules or instant espresso powder.

Cornstarch. A thickening agent made from the starch of corn. Used frequently in Asian cooking, it is added at the end to thicken sauces.

Currants. Used in the dried form, they are sometimes found along with the raisins in the grocery store; otherwise, they can be found in health food or specialty stores. Store up to one year in the freezer or refrigerator.

Flour. In this book we use all-purpose (unbleached or bleached) white flour and whole wheat flour. Store whole wheat flour in the refrigerator or freezer to prevent it from going rancid. All-purpose flour is fine stored at room temperature in an airtight container.

Garlic. Buy rock-hard heads of garlic and avoid the kinds sold in boxes. The kind called "elephant" garlic is not interchangeable with regular garlic. Store at room temperature, and when the cloves begin to soften, throw them out.

Ginger (ginger root). This tuber is used frequently as a seasoning in Asian and East Indian cooking. Buy hard, unwrinkled pieces. In the store, it is acceptable to break off a section from a large piece and buy just the small amount you need. Wrap in a paper towel and store in a plastic bag in the refrigerator. If ginger becomes moldy, throw it out.

Herbs. We use both fresh and dried, but prefer fresh herbs whenever they are available. Many markets are carrying more varieties of fresh herbs; look for them first. The general rule of thumb is to use only one-third as much dried as you would fresh.

Jalapeño chilies. Small, green, hot chili peppers used in many ethnic cuisines. Commonly sold in supermarkets as well as ethnic groceries. Look for fresh peppers with shiny, unwrinkled skins. When using in cooking, cut in half and remove seeds. These chilies are very hot; wash your hands after touching so as not to irritate your eyes. Do not confuse with serrano chilies, which are even smaller and hotter. Canned jalapeños may be substituted if the fresh are not available.

Mushrooms. Among the many varieties in the market, the most commonly available and least expensive are the white button mushrooms, but increasingly available are the brown cremini mushrooms; these can be used interchangeably. When buying mushrooms look for tightly closed caps and no soft spots. Wipe mushrooms clean with just a damp paper towel. The more exotic varieties of mushrooms—shiitake, chanterelle, morel, oyster, etc.—come in many sizes, shapes, and colors. These are generally bolder in flavor and fun to experiment with as you become more comfortable with cooking.

Nuts. To keep fresh and to prevent rancidity, keep nuts in the freezer in a tightly sealed container or freezer bags.

Oils. In this book we use vegetable oil, olive oil, and sesame oil. Vegetable oils include canola, cottonseed, corn, peanut, safflower, and soybean oil. In general their use is interchangeable, although some cooks prefer corn or peanut oil for stir-frying. Olive oil has a stronger flavor, and it is best to stock two different kinds for two different purposes: when the oil is not for cooking, find a good-quality, extra-virgin olive oil. You can pay a lot for some very exclusive (and wonderful) brands, but Bertolli makes a fine extra-virgin oil that is readily available in supermarkets. For cooking, choose an olive oil listed as simply 100 percent pure. Once again, Bertolli is a fine choice. Sesame oil is found in the Asian section of most grocery stores; this oil is used as a flavoring agent only, and not for cooking.

Onions. In general we use sweet yellow onions or red onions in these recipes. Make sure onions you buy are firm. Store, uncovered, in a dry, room-temperature environment.

Parsley. The most commonly found herb in the market comes in two varieties, curly and flat-leaf Italian. We prefer the latter.

Pepper, black. Pepper loses its flavor after being ground, so most good cooks always use freshly ground. Buy whole peppercorns and invest in a good-quality pepper mill for the kitchen and the table.

Pine nuts (pignolia or piñon nuts). Available in the specialty section of most markets. Store as you would other nuts.

Salt. For this book we have specified ordinary table salt, although we actually prefer coarse kosher salt or sea salt when they are available; these salts do not contain any additives. Because they are coarser, you may wish to use a little more.

Scallions. These are also known as green onions.

Sesame oil. See Oils.

Soy sauce. A liquid Asian condiment brewed from fermented soybeans and other ingredients. Brands vary considerably in flavor intensity and quality. The Japanese soy sauces are usually lighter than the Chinese varieties. We recommend Kikkoman, either regular or the low-sodium variety.

Spices. Most spices come in two forms, whole or ground. Read a recipe carefully to see what form is called for and the label carefully when you are buying them. Store spices away from heat and sunlight. Red spices such as paprika, cayenne, chili powder, and red pepper flakes are best stored in the refrigerator. When spices lose their fragrance, discard them.

Sugar. The various forms of sugar—granulated, powdered, brown—are not interchangeable in a recipe. Powdered sugar (also known as confectioners' sugar) is much more finely processed than granulated and has a small percentage of cornstarch added. Brown sugar comes in two forms, light and dark. Dark brown sugar has molasses added for deeper flavor, but we find either can be used in a recipe.

Sun-dried tomatoes. These are packaged in two ways, dried in plastic bags or bottled in olive oil. Either can be used in a recipe, but the dried must be soaked first in hot water for 30 minutes. Better supermarkets and specialty stores carry both types.

Tomatoes. The best bets in the market are labeled Roma, hothouse, or vine-ripened tomatoes. But most of the year, for cooking, we choose canned, Italian-style pear tomatoes, which are packed at the peak of ripeness. If you find really ripe, fresh tomatoes, use them. Cherry tomatoes, used fresh in salads, have no canned substitute.

Tomato paste. A highly concentrated tomato product. Typically found in cans or tubes.

Vanilla. Some recipes specify vanilla extract, a liquid, while others specify the whole vanilla bean. Use "pure" vanilla extract, never imitation.

Vinegar. Varieties include distilled white, cider, red wine, white wine, rice wine, balsamic, and herbed vinegars. Use the type specified in each recipe, because each has a unique flavor.

Whipping cream (heavy cream). A dairy product that contains approximately 36 percent butterfat, which allows it to be whipped. We prefer brands that are not ultrapasteurized.

Wines for cooking. When red or white wine is called for in a recipe, use a medium-priced, dry table wine. This also holds true for sherry. Under no circumstances use a product labeled "cooking wine."

Zest. The outer rind of a citrus fruit without the underlying white pith. Can be removed on a grater or with a utensil called a zester.

CULINARY TERMS AND TECHNIQUES

Bake. To cook in a heated oven.

Baste. A method of applying a liquid or fat, periodically during the roasting process, to keep surfaces moist.

Blanch. To cook foods briefly in boiling liquid, then place immediately in cold water to stop the cooking process.

Boil. To cook over high heat in rapidly rolling liquid.

Braise. To cook slowly, covered, over medium-low heat with a small amount of liquid, on top of the stove or in the oven.

Broil. To cook food using intense, overhead heat.

Brown. To cook food, usually at high temperatures, to deepen surface color. This can be done in the oven, under the broiler, or by sautéing.

Butter (grease). To spread a thin film of butter, oil, shortening, or nonstick cooking spray over the inside of a cooking vessel to prevent sticking.

Caramelize. To cook until the natural sugars in a food begin to brown visibly.

Chop. To cut food into pieces of no particular shape. Recipes will specify how finely the food should be cut.

Cream. Creaming butter means to render it into a soft, somewhat fluffy state, about the consistency of mayonnaise. The butter should be at room temperature before you begin. Frequently creaming is done at the same time the sugar is added. It can be done by hand in a bowl with a wooden spoon, but is far easier with the pastry paddle (available with some mixers) or beaters of an electric mixer. Be aggressive when creaming butter. It helps incorporate air and lighten the finished product.

Deglaze. To loosen and dissolve the browned bits from a cooking pan, by adding and boiling a small amount of liquid while scraping the inside bottom of the pan.

Degrease. To remove accumulated fat from the top of a braised, stewed, or roasted dish. This is most easily accomplished, if time allows, by refrigerating overnight and removing congealed fat the following day. Otherwise, we recommend using a gravy strainer.

Devein. To remove the ribs from the insides of bell peppers and chilies. Also refers to removing the sand vein from shrimp. Use a sharp paring knife for both.

Dice. To cut food into uniform, square shapes. Recipes will specify the size of dice.

Dredge. To cover lightly with flour. Usually done before browning meat, poultry, or fish.

Garnish. To decorate a finished plate, platter, or serving piece.

Grate. To render food into tiny particles by rubbing across any of several varieties of graters.

Grease. See Butter.

Grill. To cook on a grate over hot coals or lava rocks. Also called barbecue. Can be done indoors or outdoors. The heat source is either gas, electric, charcoal, or a specialty wood such as mesquite.

Marinate. To soak in a seasoned liquid or paste before cooking. This both tenderizes and adds flavor to the food.

Matchstick (julienne). To cut food into fine, even-sized, matchstick shapes.

Mince. To chop very finely.

Parboil. To cook food partially in a simmering liquid in preparation for some other method of cooking.

Poach. To cook over medium heat in simmering liquid.

Preheat. To bring an oven or cooking pan up to a desired temperature before adding food.

Purée. To liquefy food to a smooth consistency by using a blender, food processor, or food mill.

Roast. To cook meat, poultry, fish, or vegetables uncovered in an oven.

Sauté. To cook over medium to high heat in a small amount of hot fat. Also referred to as to fry.

Shred. To render food into long, narrow strips or ribbons by passing the food across the larger holes of a grater/shredder.

Sift. A method of lightening and evenly dispersing dry ingredients before adding to a batter. Can be accomplished with a sifter, a fine strainer, or even a fork.

Simmer. To maintain a cooking liquid so that it very slowly bubbles but does not boil rapidly.

Steam. To cook over (not in) boiling water, usually in a covered vessel, using a rack or steamer to keep food from touching the water or a double boiler with a perforated bottom.

Stir-fry. To cook over high heat with a small amount of fat in a large frying pan or wok, while stirring constantly.

Warm plates. To keep food warm or hot longer at the table. Plates can be warmed in some dishwashers, in a low oven, or by rinsing under hot water and drying before using.

Whisk. To mix liquid or dry ingredients by using a balloon-shaped utensil, usually made of wire or plastic.

How to Read a Recipe

It's simple—*read the recipe all the way through before you do anything else!*

For example, you've decided to make a cake from our book, or any cookbook, and you are all ready to start, but you discover the recipe requires butter "at room temperature," and yours is in the refrigerator—ice cold. You can soften it in your microwave, but the texture changes a bit when you do. Then, you find, after you start mixing the batter, that you don't have the right size or type of baking pan. Now what?

Believe us, these mishaps can be extremely frustrating, but we've all experienced them one time or another—actually more than once.

First, read the list of ingredients to make sure that you do have all the items and in sufficient quantity for the recipe. Read the list carefully because some spices and flavorings come in different forms. For instance, prepared mustard is a sauce and dried mustard is a powder; whole cloves (those cute things they stick in baked hams) differ from ground cloves; baking soda and baking powder are not interchangeable. See what we mean?

We recommend that you gather all the ingredients together, measure them out, and have them near your work space. We still remember the chocolate cake that became chewy brownies because the cook forgot the baking powder. Once the batter is in the oven, it's too late to add anything.

Next, read the instructions for preparation all the way through. Be sure you understand what steps are required, what procedures are necessary, what equipment you need, and in what order the recipe should be put together. We have organized our recipe directions in sequential order. If you happen on a recipe elsewhere that doesn't follow that scheme, make notations for yourself, right on the recipe page. Show us a spotless cookbook, and we'll show you someone who only eats out! In our cookbook collection, you can always tell our favorite recipes because they have some of the ingredients spilled on them and comments all over the page.

Now you have it—read the recipe first; check ingredients, amounts, equipment needed, procedures, order of putting the dish together, preparation time, including baking or cooking time. You will have great results and gain confidence in your ability. That's what this book is all about.

Starters, Soups, and Salads

Foods at their simplest—for appetizers, luncheons, and little meals

HERBED CHICKPEA DIP

This recipe is a variation on what you might know as hummus, a traditional Lebanese spread served with pita bread. It's a simple appetizer to make ahead and serve accompanied with warmed pita bread and/or raw vegetables. The best and easiest way to make this dip is in a food processor. A blender will work, but not nearly as easily. The flavors come together better if this dip is made a few hours ahead or the day before serving.

$\frac{1}{4}$ cup packed fresh parsley leaves

2 cloves garlic, peeled

1 can (15 ounces) chickpeas (garbanzo beans)

$\frac{1}{2}$ cup tahini (sesame seed paste)

$\frac{1}{2}$ teaspoon salt

$\frac{1}{2}$ cup freshly squeezed lemon juice (about 2 to 3 lemons)

In the bowl of a food processor or in a blender, combine parsley and garlic; process until finely minced. Leaving chickpeas in the can, drain the liquid from can. Fill can with cold water, then drain chickpeas again. Add chickpeas, tahini, salt, and lemon juice to the minced garlic mixture. Process the mixture to a smooth purée. Place dip in a serving bowl, cover, and refrigerate. Remove from refrigerator $\frac{1}{2}$ hour before serving.

Makes about 2 cups, serves 8 to 10.

< Nachos with Salsa, Chicken Stock

Cook's Notes

- ◆ Chickpeas are also known as garbanzo beans; look for either name on the can.
- ◆ Tahini is ground sesame seed paste, typically available in the health food section of your grocery store. Sometimes oil settles to the top of the jar; this needs to be mixed back into the paste before using. Store leftover tahini in the refrigerator; it seems to keep indefinitely when tightly sealed.
- ◆ Cut fresh pita bread into wedges, enclose in aluminum foil, and warm for 10 to 15 minutes in a preheated 250°F oven.
- ◆ Fresh vegetables such as carrots, celery, and red and green bell peppers, cut into strips, make nice accompaniments to the dip. Broccoli and cauliflower florets are also great.

NACHOS WITH SALSA

This recipe for nachos is totally adaptable. Use whatever proportions you like; these recipe amounts are just a suggestion. If you like more cheese, add it; if you like more or fewer chilies, adjust the amounts. If you prefer nachos without refried beans, skip the beans. Nachos are great to serve to a crowd, so double the recipe. Or make them just for two by halving the recipe, and then serve along with soup for dinner.

8 ounces (typically $\frac{1}{2}$ bag) tortilla chips

1 can (8 ounces) refried beans

1 can (2$\frac{1}{2}$ ounces) diced green jalapeño chilies, drained

8 ounces sharp Cheddar cheese, freshly shredded

Salsa, following

Preheat oven to 450°F. Spread tortilla chips evenly onto a cookie sheet with sides or an ovenproof platter. Using a rubber spatula or table knife, spread refried beans on the chips. Spread chilies over beans and chips, then distribute cheese evenly on top. Bake until the cheese is melted, 5 to 10 minutes. Serve hot.

Serves 4 to 6.

Cook's Notes

◆ Using 1 or 2 fresh jalapeño chilies instead of canned is an alternative for those who like really spicy foods. Slice off stem end, remove seeds, and slice into rounds. Proceed according to the directions.

◆ Use 8 ounces of Monterey jack or pepper-jack cheese instead of Cheddar cheese.

◆ Add freshly diced avocado to the nachos just before serving.

Salsa

A favorite accompaniment to nachos, and so easy to make. If you like your salsa chunky, then chop the ingredients by hand. If you prefer a smoother salsa, put everything in a food processor. Salsa will keep well for three or four days tightly covered under refrigeration.

4 ripe tomatoes (about 1 pound), diced

½ small yellow onion (about 2 ounces), peeled and diced

2 fresh jalapeño chilies, seeded and minced

¼ cup fresh cilantro leaves, chopped

1 tablespoon freshly squeezed lime juice

½ teaspoon salt

In a bowl, stir together all ingredients, mixing well. Cover and refrigerate until serving time.

Makes about 1½ cups.

Cook's Notes

◆ For those who prefer their salsa hot, include the seeds from the jalapeños as well. Be sure to wash your hands immediately after handling chilies, so you will not inadvertently touch and irritate your eyes.

Eggplant Dip with Garlic and Olive Oil

Baking an eggplant gives it a distinctive smoky flavor. This dip is tangy and a little spicy, and can also be used as a salsa to serve with hamburgers or other meat dishes. Even people who say they don't like eggplant will find it tasty. This dip can be served with other raw vegetables for dunking, but it is best with crackers, pieces of French bread, or wedges of pita bread.

1 medium eggplant (about 1 pound)

2 cloves garlic, peeled and pressed

½ jalapeño chili, seeded, deveined, and minced

4 scallions, white part and about 1 inch of green tops, thinly sliced

2 to 3 tablespoons minced fresh parsley

1 medium-size fresh tomato, peeled and diced

2 tablespoons plain yogurt

1 tablespoon olive oil

Salt and freshly ground black pepper, to taste

Preheat oven to 375°F. Place eggplant on a double sheet of aluminum foil and prick skin in several places with a fork. Bake until eggplant feels soft when pressed with a finger, 60 to 70 minutes. Remove and let cool until you can handle it without burning your hands.

Place eggplant in a large mixing bowl. Remove and discard the peel and mash the insides. Mix in the remaining ingredients, and refrigerate several hours before serving to allow the flavor to blend. Adjust the seasonings if needed. *Makes about 2 cups.*

Cook's Notes

◆ **Use a sheet of aluminum foil to bake the eggplant and you won't have a dirty pan to wash. Be sure to prick the eggplant in several places with a fork before baking so it doesn't explode in the oven.**

CROSTINI

Crostini is a fancy word for little toasts spread with flavored butters, or topped with marinated vegetables, or crowned with sliced cheeses and garnish. Your imagination is your guide. Here is a basic method for preparing the toasts and some suggested toppings for appetizers. Use the baguette-shaped loaves of French bread.

1/4-inch-thick slices crusty French bread (about 4 slices per person)
Olive oil, for brushing

Slices of "fresh" mozzarella cheese (see Cook's Notes) topped with oil-packed sun-dried tomatoes
Spreadable goat cheese
1/2 stick (4 tablespoons) unsalted butter, at room temperature, blended with 1 tablespoon anchovy paste
1/2 cup cream cheese, at room temperature, blended with 1/4 cup chopped fresh herbs such as basil, tarragon, parsley, or dill

Preheat oven to 350°F. Brush both sides of bread rounds with olive oil. Spread in a single layer on a baking sheet and bake until lightly brown on one side, 10 to 15 minutes. Turn and bake until lightly brown on the other side, 10 to 15 minutes. Toasts should be crunchy but not brittle. Arrange on a serving platter with assorted toppings. *Allow 4 slices per person.*

Cook's Notes

◆ **"Fresh" mozzarella refers to the type that is usually ball-shaped and stored in water in the deli case at better cheese retailers. It has a different taste and texture than the packaged variety.**

◆ **Greek-style olive and eggplant spreads in jars can often be found in better stores, and make easy crostini toppings.**

◆ **Remember to have toppings based on butter or cheeses at room temperature; they will spread easier and have more pronounced flavor.**

◆ **Toasts may be prepared in advance and stored in tightly sealed plastic bags for up to 2 days.**

CHICKEN STOCK

Homemade chicken stock (broth) is an absolute snap to make. Nothing quite like it comes from a can, and good stock is the single most important ingredient in many soups and sauces. It just takes its time gently bubbling away on the stovetop, producing wonderfully flavorful liquid from pieces like necks, gizzards, back and rib bones, and wing tips—all most likely to be otherwise thrown away. Start today to develop a very smart habit: Store necks, tails, wing tips, gizzards, hearts, backs, rib (breast) bones—anything except livers—in a gallon-size reclosable freezer bag in your freezer. When the bag is really full, you have enough chicken parts to make a small pot of homemade stock. Squeeze excess air out of the bag each time you add chicken pieces; this helps to prevent dehydration known as "freezer burn." There are several time-honored methods of making chicken stock. Here is our simple approach to a basic stock that can be used for Western-style or Asian cooking.

4 quarts (about 4 pounds) chicken parts

Western Seasonings

1 medium unpeeled carrot

1 medium unpeeled yellow onion

1/2 rib celery, with leaves

1/2 teaspoon whole black peppercorns

1 bay leaf

1 cup loosely packed parsley leaves and stems

Asian Seasonings

4 unpeeled cloves garlic

4 whole scallions with green tops

3 slices (about the size of a quarter) unpeeled fresh ginger root

Select a heavy 4-quart saucepan or a 6- to 8-quart stockpot. Fill it almost to the top with raw chicken parts and cover with cold water, leaving 2 inches of space at the top of the pan. Bring the water to a boil over medium-high heat and reduce heat so that the liquid simmers steadily. Skim off the brown foam rising to the top, using a soup skimmer, small tea strainer, or serving spoon. After 5 minutes or so the foam will become white; no more skimming is necessary.

Add Western or Asian seasonings if desired. Cover pot loosely and regulate the heat so that the liquid just barely simmers. Simmer the stock for 4 to 8 hours, adding water if necessary to keep the bones covered.

Remove bones and meat, draining them thoroughly in a colander or strainer set over a large bowl to catch all the juices. Discard bones and meat and pour the collected drippings into the stockpot. Pour the stock through a fine strainer into the large bowl, then back into the stockpot. Set the pot into a sink filled with cold water, changing the water after 10 minutes and again after 20 minutes. Cover the pot and refrigerate overnight.

Before using the stock, scrape the congealed fat from the surface using a slotted or large serving spoon. The stock is now ready to use. If the stock is needed immediately after it is made, use a gravy strainer or a wide, shallow spoon (held just under the surface) to remove the liquid fat.

Makes 3 to 6 quarts.

Homemade Chicken Soup

In a 3-quart saucepan over medium heat, sauté 1 small sliced onion, 1 small sliced carrot, and 1 rib sliced celery in 2 tablespoons butter until the onion is soft, about 5 minutes. Pour in 2 quarts homemade chicken stock, add ½ teaspoon dried thyme, several sprigs parsley, and a few grinds black pepper. Simmer until the vegetables are soft but not mushy, about 20 minutes. Taste for salt, adding as much as necessary to brighten flavor without making the soup "salty." Add 1 or 2 cups diced leftover chicken, and, if you like, stir in a couple of cups of cooked rice or noodles.

Serves 4 to 6.

Cook's Notes

- **Canned chicken broth is a time saver as a substitute for fresh chicken stock, and we often do use it. Buy the low-sodium variety, if available. Read the ingredient list and buy a brand without MSG, if possible. *Always* taste what you are serving before adding salt when using canned broth; it has plenty of salt already added, so using more before tasting can lead to disaster. If you are reducing (boiling down) a liquid that includes canned broth, remember that you are increasing its salty taste as well.**

- **To save homemade stock: Refrigerate up to 3 to 4 days. If not used, reboil for 5 minutes, cool, and refrigerate again. Or freeze in a large, tightly covered container (if using**

glass with screw-on lids always leave 1 or 2 inches of space at the top). Or pour into ice cube trays, freeze, and cover tightly; this allows you to add small amounts of quality stock to dishes you are preparing later with no added work.

TOMATO SOUP

This recipe is what real tomato soup should taste like. Most of us grew up on cream of tomato soup coming out of a red-and-white-labeled can. We think you will be wonderfully surprised when you taste the difference—it made us all want to have the soup in a mug, in front of a glowing hot fire. For a casual dinner with friends, make a salad, buy some hearty bread, and enjoy a bowl of soup. For a low-fat variation, substitute plain low-fat yogurt for the cream. The yogurt gives the soup a wonderfully tangy quality.

    3 tablespoons olive oil
    1 medium-size yellow onion (about ½ pound), peeled and chopped
    2 medium cloves garlic, peeled and minced
    3 cups Chicken Stock (page 32) or canned low-sodium chicken broth
    2 cans (28 ounces each) peeled Italian pear tomatoes with liquid
    1 cup whipping cream or plain low-fat yogurt
    1 teaspoon salt
    1½ teaspoons granulated sugar
    ¼ teaspoon freshly ground black pepper

Using a heavy 3½- to 4-quart saucepan, heat olive oil over medium heat for about 30 seconds. Add onion and garlic and sauté for 5 minutes. (Turn down heat if onion and garlic are browning.) Add chicken broth and tomatoes with their liquid. Turn up heat until the liquids begin to boil. Now turn down heat so that soup just simmers and cook uncovered for 15 minutes. Remove from heat and cool slightly.

Purée soup in batches in a blender. You will need a bowl to hold the puréed soup while you are completing the batches. Pour all of the puréed soup back in the pan and add cream or yogurt, salt, sugar, and pepper. Stir to blend the soup, and taste. Heat the soup, but do not let it boil. Serve in mugs or bowls. This soup keeps well up to 1 week, tightly covered in the refrigerator.

Makes about 10 cups, serves 6 to 8.

Cook's Notes

◆ **We hauled out a 13-year-old avocado-green blender to purée this soup! Fancy equipment is not required. We actually prefer to use a blender for this particular task because we tend to overfill a food processor, which results in soup leaking out of the bottom of the container when it is removed from the base of the machine!**

◆ **Basil is often added to canned peeled Italian pear tomatoes, but that's OK for this recipe.**

NEW ENGLAND CLAM CHOWDER

If you have only eaten clam chowder in a restaurant, you will probably be surprised that this one is not thick. Restaurants have to thicken the soup in order to "hold" it in the steam table. True New England clam chowder, however, is thickened only by the starch from the potatoes. The recipe calls for milk but you can also use half-and-half, which makes the soup thicker and adds a wonderful flavor. The authentic recipe cooks the onions in the fat from the bacon, but we only ask for about a teaspoon for flavor.

20 medium clams in shells or 2 cans (6 ½ ounces each) chopped
  clams with liquid
6 strips bacon
1 medium-size yellow onion (about 5 ounces), peeled and diced
1 tablespoon unsalted butter
2 medium-size russet potatoes (about 1 pound total), peeled and diced
2 cups milk or half-and-half
Salt (optional) and freshly ground black pepper, to taste
½ cup minced fresh parsley

If you are using fresh clams, scrub the shells well with a stiff brush and discard any that are opened. Place clams in a 6-quart stockpot, cover with cold water, and bring to a boil. Cook until they all open, 5 to 10 minutes; discard any clams that do not open. Remove clams and strain the liquid into a bowl and set it aside. Remove clams from shell, chop, and set them aside. If you are using canned clams, just open the cans and drain the liquid into a bowl and set it aside.

In a heavy 4-quart saucepan, cook bacon over medium heat until crisp. Drain on paper towels and crumble. Remove all bacon fat from the pan except about a teaspoon. Add butter to the pan, melt over medium heat, add onions, and cook until they are translucent, about 5 minutes.

Measure out 2 cups of the reserved clam liquid and add to onions with potatoes. (If you use canned clams, add water to the liquid from the can to make 2 cups.) Bring to a boil, reduce heat to simmer, and cook until the potatoes are tender, about 30 minutes. Add milk, chopped clams, and crumbled bacon pieces; and cook just until heated through. Add pepper and taste to see if you wish to add salt, but clams are salty and usually the soup doesn't need any. Ladle soup into individual bowls and garnish with parsley.
Serves 4 to 6.

Cook's Notes

◆ **If using canned clams, you may add bottled clam juice, instead of water, to make 2 cups liquid. The flavor will be more intense.**

POTATO SOUP

This is one of the simplest yet most satisfying soups we could offer you. It's easy to make, freezes well, and lends itself to nice variations. It also goes awfully well with our tuna salad!

2 tablespoons unsalted butter
1 large yellow onion (10 to 12 ounces), peeled and coarsely chopped
3 or 4 large russet potatoes (2 to 2½ pounds), peeled and cut
    into 6 to 8 pieces each
4 cans (14½ ounces each) low-sodium chicken broth

4 or 5 sprigs fresh thyme or ¾ teaspoon dried thyme
2 or 3 sprigs fresh parsley
A few grinds black pepper
Salt to taste (about 2 teaspoons)
½ cup chopped fresh parsley
¼ cup chopped fresh oregano

In a heavy 4-quart saucepan, melt butter, add onion, and sauté over medium heat until onion is soft but not browned, about 5 minutes. Add potatoes, broth, thyme, and parsley sprigs. Bring to a boil, reduce to a simmer, cover, and cook until potatoes are tender when pierced with a fork, 15 to 18 minutes.

Drain potatoes into a bowl, saving the liquid. Remove thyme and parsley sprigs. Purée the solids in 2 batches in a blender or food processor, adding potato liquid as necessary. Return pureed vegetables and reserved cooking liquid to pan. Season with pepper and taste for salt, adding as desired. Stir in chopped parsley and oregano just before serving.
Serves 8 to 10.

Cook's Notes

◆ **Substitute 1¾ cups milk or whipping cream for 1 can of the chicken broth for extra richness. If using milk, don't boil. Try adding broccoli florets, thick fresh mushroom slices, washed spinach leaves, chunks of fresh asparagus, etc. Cook them in the puréed potato base until as tender as you wish.**

◆ **Avoid using dried oregano to garnish this soup. If you can't obtain fresh oregano, substitute fresh parsley.**

ITALIAN VEGETABLE AND BEAN SOUP WITH PESTO

We believe that food should please the eye as well as the taste buds. You may use any variation of vegetables you wish. This combination is suggested for color and taste. We used two kinds of beans and two varieties of squash for both reasons. Letting the soup stand for thirty minutes allows the flavors to mingle and ingredients to finish cooking without becoming overdone.

3 tablespoons Pesto, following

¼ cup olive oil

2 cloves garlic, peeled and pressed into the oil with a garlic press

2 leeks with about 2 inches green tops, thinly sliced

2 carrots, sliced in thin rounds

1 small zucchini (about 5 ounces), cut into ½-inch dice

1 red bell pepper, seeded, deveined, and sliced into thin matchstick strips

3 ribs celery with leaves, sliced

2 cans (14½ ounces each) beef broth plus 2 cups water, or
    6 cups water instead of broth

1 can (14½ ounces) peeled, chopped tomatoes with liquid

1 package (9 ounces) frozen Italian green beans, thawed

1½ cups peeled, seeded, and diced winter squash (hubbard,
    butternut, etc.)

1 can (15 ounces) cannellini or small white beans, drained and
    rinsed lightly

½ cup small dried macaroni, such as elbows or shells

½ cup minced fresh parsley

Salt and freshly ground black pepper, to taste

Prepare Pesto and set aside. In a 6-quart stockpot, heat oil and garlic over medium heat; sauté leeks, carrots, zucchini, bell pepper, and celery until slightly tender, about 5 minutes. Add broth, water, and tomatoes. Bring to a boil, reduce heat, cover, and simmer for 30 minutes. Add green beans, winter squash, cannellini beans, and macaroni. Continue cooking for 10 minutes more. Remove from heat and add Pesto and parsley, stirring to distribute well. Add salt and pepper. Let stand, covered, for 20 to 30 minutes before serving.
Serves 6 to 8.

Pesto

2 cups fresh basil leaves

½ cup good-quality olive oil

2 tablespoons toasted pine nuts (see Cook's Notes)

4 cloves garlic, peeled and minced

1 teaspoon salt

½ cup freshly grated Parmesan cheese

Place basil, olive oil, pine nuts, and garlic in a blender or food processor. Blend until smooth. Pour into a small bowl and add salt and cheese. Pesto can be stored in a covered jar in the refrigerator up to 2 weeks, or frozen. It will keep frozen for several months.
Makes 1 cup.

Cook's Notes

◆　**If you can't find frozen Italian green beans, which are wider than regular green beans, use cut green beans instead. Do not, however, use French-cut green beans, because they** will cook away. You can, of course, use fresh green beans if they are in season.

- ◆ To toast pine nuts, heat a small, heavy-bottomed frying pan over medium-high heat; when hot, add pine nuts and stir constantly until lightly browned. Remove to a plate to cool.
- ◆ This soup freezes beautifully.

CREAMY ONION SOUP

This gutsy, richly flavored soup is wonderful in the fall and winter. Typically, onion soup is made with beef stock, but in this preparation we prefer to use a combination of beef and chicken stock, which lends a better balance to the flavors. If you prefer to save some calories, substitute plain low-fat yogurt for the whipping cream and omit the lemon juice. The yogurt will give the soup enough tang. Served with hearty bread and a salad, this makes a great fireside supper.

1 stick (^{1}/4 pound) unsalted butter

5 large yellow onions (3 to 3^1/2 pounds), peeled and chopped

2 cloves garlic, peeled and minced

3 tablespoons all-purpose flour

2 cups canned beef broth

1 cup Chicken Stock (page 32) or canned low-sodium chicken broth

1 cup water

1 teaspoon salt

Freshly ground black pepper, to taste (3 or 4 grinds)

^{1}/2 cup whipping cream

1 tablespoon freshly squeezed lemon juice

In a 3^1/2 to 4-quart heavy saucepan or Dutch oven, heat

butter over medium heat until melted. Add onion and garlic. Sauté, stirring frequently, until soft, about 5 minutes. Turn heat to low, cover pan, and continue cooking for an additional 25 minutes. Check frequently to be sure the mixture is not burning.

Turn up heat to medium high, sprinkle flour over onions, and stir to combine. (Make sure all lumps are smoothed out of flour.) Now add beef broth, chicken stock, and the water. Stir to combine, then add salt and pepper. Bring to a boil, reduce heat to maintain a simmer, cover, and cook an additional 30 minutes.

Just before serving, add whipping cream and lemon juice. Taste the soup, and adjust the flavors by adding more salt or pepper, if desired.
Serves 6 to 8.

Cook's Notes

- ◆ **Freeze any leftover broth for use in future recipes. Small quantities of broth are great to have on hand for stir-fry recipes.**
- ◆ **This soup can be made 2 to 3 days before you are planning to serve it. Keep tightly covered in the refrigerator.**

TIPS ON MAKING GREEN SALADS

The fundamentals of making a good green salad require fresh, interesting greens and a good quality dressing. To our way of thinking, the only good dressing is homemade. Once you discover how easy it is to make your own dressing, hopefully, the bottled types will be a distant memory.

Select fresh greens without brown spots or "burnt" edges if possible. Try to buy lettuces that look crisp and moist, not wilted and dry. Smaller lettuce heads tend to be younger and less bitter near the core than gargantuan heads. We're fondest of leaf lettuce (red and green), romaine, butter lettuce, escarole (with its own desirable bitterness), and spinach. Iceberg lettuce is usually crisp but lacks the flavor of these other varieties; we're most likely to use it as a shredded garnish for dishes such as enchiladas or burritos. You'll need to experiment with the greens available in your region to find your favorites.

To prepare the greens, separate the leaves from whatever white, inner core may exist. Rinse them under cold running water or swish them in a clean sink full of cold water to allow the sandy grit to fall to the bottom, and drain well. Tear the leaves into bite-size pieces (either before or after drying them) and be certain to dry them well. We prefer to use a salad spinner, but you can pat leaves dry on paper toweling if you like. Cleaned dry lettuces will keep well for two or three days when packed into a large plastic bag along with a paper towel to absorb excess moisture.

A good salad dressing consists of an appealing blend of fat and acid—in other words, oil and vinegar (or citrus juice)—and seasonings. The vinegars that are best for salads, in our opinion, are rice vinegar, white wine vinegar, red wine vinegar, and balsamic vinegar. Rice vinegar is light-colored and mild, often found in the Asian foods section of your market. White wine vinegar is a little more acidic usually, often found flavored with fresh or dried herbs. Red wine vinegar is a little more assertive yet, and is sometimes sold flavored with herbs. (There is nothing inherently wrong with a flavored vinegar so long as the flavoring fits into the cook's overall plan.) Balsamic is a white wine vinegar aged a long time in casks so that it becomes dark red in appearance and is especially mellow. (Note to dieters: A little sprinkling of balsamic vinegar alone makes an acceptable dressing on greens or vegetables.)

Plain vegetable oil—"salad" oil—works to make a salad dressing, but olive oil packs a lot more flavor. "Extra-virgin" grade costs a bit more than "pure" grade olive oil, but is worth it; it has a more delicate, less acidic, flavor. Supermarket brands such as Bertolli now offer extra-virgin grade olive oil, while specialty food stores may offer you a shelf-full of different brands to taste, many of them quite expensive. Please your taste buds and your wallet and buy the brand you like best. Life is full of pleasant decisions to make!

THE PURIST'S GREEN SALAD

A great salad doesn't need a lot of stuff in it. In fact, simplicity, with the emphasis on high-quality ingredients, is what is suggested here. This dressing is wonderfully balanced and very versatile. Several variations are offered in the Cook's Notes.

Dressing

2 tablespoons rice wine vinegar or balsamic vinegar

6 tablespoons extra-virgin olive oil

$1/4$ teaspoon granulated sugar

$1/4$ teaspoon salt

Freshly ground black pepper, to taste

$1 1/2$ tablespoons minced fresh parsley

8 medium-size fresh mushrooms, wiped clean with a damp paper towel, then thinly sliced

1 large head lettuce (leaf, red leaf, romaine, or a mixture), cleaned and dried (see Cook's Notes)

In a large bowl (the bigger the better, since you have to toss the lettuce in here), mix vinegar, olive oil, sugar, salt, and pepper. Stir well to combine. Add minced parsley. Mix well and taste. Adjust the seasonings to taste.

About 20 minutes before serving, add sliced mushrooms to the dressing. Toss well and let marinate. When ready to serve the salad, tear lettuce into bite-size pieces and add to the bowl. Toss to combine. Divide among salad plates and serve immediately.

Serves 6.

Cook's Notes

◆ **For the amount of dressing specified in this recipe, about 8 cups of lightly packed salad greens is the amount you will need. When first learning to make good salads, it really is helpful to measure the amount of greens—after a while you won't bother, your trained eye will know!**

Variations

Curried dressing. Use rice wine vinegar and add $1/2$ teaspoon curry powder to the dressing.

Garlic dressing. Use rice wine vinegar and add $1/4$ teaspoon minced garlic to the dressing.

Basil dressing. Substitute freshly minced basil for the parsley, or use half basil and half parsley.

Creamy dressing. Using rice wine vinegar and add 1 tablespoon whipping cream to the dressing. Blend well to combine.

EVERYTHING BUT THE KITCHEN SINK SALAD

Here is a recipe for the person who likes salad with lots of "stuff" in it. Pick and choose among our long list of possibilities. Be sure to read Tips on Making Green Salads (page 38) for a full explanation of preparing salad greens and a discussion of making salad dressing.

Dressing

2 tablespoons red or white wine vinegar

$1/2$ cup extra-virgin olive oil

1 teaspoon Dijon-style mustard

$1/2$ teaspoon granulated sugar

$1/4$ teaspoon salt

Freshly ground black pepper, to taste

$1 1/2$ tablespoons minced fresh parsley

1 to 2 cups of a mixture of any or all, of the following: sliced scallions, grated carrot, sprouts, tomato wedges, sliced mushrooms, sliced black olives, thinly sliced red onion, shredded red cabbage, diced celery, sliced cucumber, sliced radishes, marinated artichoke hearts, croutons, bacon bits, sliced hard-cooked eggs, diced avocados, thawed frozen peas, sunflower seeds, or bite-size florets of raw broccoli or cauliflower

8 cups lightly packed salad greens, cleaned and dried. Choose any, all, or a combination of the following: leaf lettuce, red leaf lettuce, romaine, escarole, spinach, endive, butter lettuce, limestone lettuce, arugula, lamb's lettuce, or any other edible green.

In a large bowl (the bigger the better, since you have to toss the lettuce in here) mix vinegar, olive oil, mustard, sugar, salt, and pepper. Stir well to combine. Add minced parsley. Mix well and adjust seasonings to taste.

About 20 minutes before serving add the 1 to 2 cups of mixed vegetables, etc. (except croutons and sunflower seeds) to the dressing. Toss well and let marinate. When ready to serve, tear the lettuce into bite-size pieces and add to the bowl. Add croutons and/or sunflower seeds, if using. Toss to combine. Divide among salad plates and serve immediately. *Serves 6 to 8.*

COLESLAW

Good American food, coleslaw is unfussy and always a welcome addition to a meal of burgers, ribs, hot dogs, or any other soul-satisfying foods. *We have chosen a lightly creamy-style slaw as our basic with a variation of an oil and vinegar dressing. This is an easy recipe to double to take to a potluck.*

1 pound green cabbage (about $\frac{1}{2}$ medium head)

3 scallions with about 1 inch green top, thinly sliced

$\frac{1}{2}$ cup chopped fresh parsley

Dressing

$\frac{1}{3}$ cup mayonnaise

$\frac{1}{4}$ cup buttermilk

$1\frac{1}{2}$ teaspoons red wine vinegar

$1\frac{1}{2}$ teaspoon dried dill weed

2 teaspoons Dijon-style mustard

1 dash hot pepper sauce

$\frac{1}{4}$ teaspoon granulated sugar

Salt and freshly ground black pepper, to taste

Remove any tough, outer leaves from the head of cabbage, rinse it, and drain. Using a chef's knife, cut head in quarters and place on cutting board. Remove white center core and discard, then cut cabbage in thin shreds, about $\frac{1}{4}$ inch thick or less. Place cabbage in a large mixing bowl and add sliced scallions and chopped parsley.

Mix all the dressing ingredients in a separate bowl, blend with a whisk, and then pour over cabbage. Toss well. Cover and refrigerate for a few hours before serving. (We like our slaw well chilled.) *Serves 6.*

- We prefer the texture of coleslaw whose cabbage is cut by hand with a chef's knife. You can use a hand grater or the grater attachment to a food processor, but we think this makes a watery product.
- Toss cabbage, scallions, and parsley mixture with your favorite oil and vinegar dressing. Particularly good are those made with a quality red wine vinegar and a pinch of sugar.

POTATO SALAD

Here's a classic potato salad—simple, easy to make ahead, great for a family, and readily doubled or even tripled for a crowd. It's a perfect accompaniment to grilled burgers or spareribs in the summer and to a good corned beef sandwich or meatloaf sandwich in the winter.

4 large red potatoes (about 1½ pounds)

2 large hard-cooked eggs, peeled and chopped

¼ cup diced scallions with about 2 inches green part

1 large green or red bell pepper (about 8 ounces), seeded, deveined, and cut into ½-inch dice

1 cup mayonnaise

½ teaspoon salt

½ teaspoon freshly ground black pepper

Peel potatoes and rinse them. Place in a 3- to 4-quart saucepan and cover with cold water. Bring to a boil, reduce heat, and simmer until potatoes feel tender but not mushy when pierced with a knife, 25 to 30 minutes. Drain potatoes and let them cool.

In the meantime, combine eggs, scallions, bell pepper, mayonnaise, salt, and pepper in a large mixing bowl. Cut potatoes into 1-inch cubes. Combine with the other ingredients and stir gently but thoroughly to mix. Cover and refrigerate until ready to serve.

Makes about 7 cups, serves 6 to 8.

Cook's Notes

- Be sure to keep this salad cold until serving time. Mayonnaise-based salads, along with eggs, are very susceptible to growth of bacteria that cause food poisoning. Do not leave it in the sun or on a buffet for hours.
- If you don't like onion in your potato salad, then leave it out. If you like more crunch than just green pepper, add ¼ cup diced celery.
- If you like your potato salad to have some kick, add ¼ teaspoon cayenne or a dash of hot pepper sauce.

TUNA SALAD

We, like most people, love tuna salad. It's a comfort food for most of us, whether sandwiched between two slabs of bread or arranged handsomely in a nest of butter lettuce garnished with tomato wedges. We prefer ours with a little crunch in the chew, hence the celery and onion. If you can, make it the day you want to eat it and chill an hour or two. It lasts several days in the refrigerator, but a little moisture will separate out.

2 cans (6⅛ ounces each) solid white tuna (oil or water packed)
1 rib celery, finely diced
⅓ cup peeled and finely diced red onion
2 tablespoons dill pickle relish
1 hard-cooked egg, peeled and coarsely grated or chopped
A few grinds black pepper
½ teaspoon dried dill weed
About ½ cup mayonnaise

Drain tuna thoroughly. In a medium bowl gently flake tuna with a fork without mashing. Add remaining ingredients except mayonnaise and toss together. Add just enough mayonnaise to moisten and blend well.
Makes 2 large salads, 3 to 4 small salads, or 4 sandwiches.

CHINESE NOODLE SALAD

Our modern American culture continues to incorporate foods from around the world into a basic repertoire. A recent example is cold Chinese noodles, variations of which can now be found in delis around the country. There is good reason for the popularity of this dish from our Asian friends. These noodles are easy to make, and they are healthy since they incorporate current guidelines about low-fat, high-carbohydrate eating. This is our version. The recipe doubles easily if you want to take it to a potluck.

4 to 6 quarts water
½ pound dried thin spaghetti noodles
1 tablespoon salt
1 tablespoon sesame seeds
1 medium carrot, peeled and finely grated
3 medium scallions with 1 inch green part thinly sliced
¼ cup vegetable oil
2 tablespoons peanut butter, smooth or chunky
1 tablespoon sesame oil
1 tablespoon unseasoned rice wine vinegar or white vinegar
2 tablespoons soy sauce
¼ teaspoon (or to taste) Chinese hot chili sauce (see Cook's Notes)

Bring the water to a boil in a large saucepan or stockpot and toss in salt. Add spaghetti and cook until tender but with still some bite (al dente). Drain in a colander and rinse pasta under cold running water. Set aside.

In a small frying pan, toast sesame seeds over medium heat until brown, shaking frequently. Remove from heat and set aside.

In a large mixing bowl, combine carrots, scallions, and drained noodles. In a small bowl, using a whisk, mix all the remaining ingredients until well blended. Pour over noodles and toss well. (We think it is easiest to do this with your hands; just be sure they are very clean.) Cover noodles and refrigerate for several hours or overnight. Just before serving toss with the toasted sesame seeds.

These noodles will last refrigerated for up to a week and, if anything, just get better.
Serves 4.

- Chinese hot chili sauce is a bright-tasting, thick sauce found in cans in Asian grocery stores. If you don't have time to get to a specialty market, substitute an equal amount of Tabasco or other hot pepper sauce.
- Reserve a few of the toasted sesame seeds or some additional scallion rings to sprinkle over the completed salad for a pleasant garnish.

PASTA SALAD

There are probably as many variations of pasta salad as there are cookbooks written. We offer you a version that is not dependent on seasonal produce. We have tried to keep the list of ingredients short, yet the tastes exciting. If you are not familiar with capers or sun-dried tomatoes, this salad will give you a good introduction. Commonly found on the grocer's shelf, both of these ingredients are wonderful to have on hand for other pasta dishes, hot or cold. If you are cooking for a crowd, double the recipe; otherwise, serve as few as two and enjoy the leftovers. This salad is best made at least two hours before serving, or make a day ahead.

$1/2$ pound dried pasta (penne, rotini, bow-ties, or sea shells)
1 medium-size red bell pepper, seeded, deveined, and cut into
$1/2$-inch dice
$1/4$ cup thinly sliced scallion with about 2 inches green part
$1/4$ cup minced fresh parsley
$1/2$ cup frozen peas, rinsed under hot water, then drained
1 tablespoon capers, rinsed and drained
$1/4$ cup thinly sliced sun-dried tomatoes (see Cook's Notes)

Dressing

3 tablespoons rice wine vinegar
6 tablespoons extra-virgin olive oil
1 teaspoon salt
1 teaspoon granulated sugar
$1/2$ teaspoon freshly ground black pepper

Cook pasta according to the directions on page 65. Drain in a colander, then rinse under cold water. Shake all excess water from the pasta, otherwise the water will dilute the dressing. In a large mixing bowl combine pasta, bell pepper, scallion, parsley, peas, capers, and tomatoes. Mix to combine.

In a glass measuring cup or small bowl, combine the dressing ingredients. Stir well, then pour over the pasta mixture. Mix to combine. Cover and refrigerate. Remove to room temperature $1/2$ hour before serving.
Serves 6.

Cook's Notes

- Sun-dried tomatoes are available either packed in oil or packaged in dried form. Our preference for this recipe is the type packed in oil. Include any of the oil clinging to the tomatoes as you measure and chop; it will just add to the flavor.

< Chinese Noodle Salad

- There is no need to cook the peas. Rinsing under hot water will begin the thawing process and by the time the salad is completed the peas will be fully thawed.

- In summer, substitute fresh basil for the parsley and use vine-ripened tomatoes for the sun-dried ones. If a fresh vegetable looks appealing at the market, substitute it for the peas or add in addition to them. Blanch (see page 85-86) fresh vegetables such as asparagus, broccoli, or cauliflower before adding to the salad. Zucchini and yellow squash are fine to use raw.

- If you would like to make this salad a main course, you could add cooked fresh baby shrimp, diced cooked chicken, or matchstick-cut roast beef. Canned tuna, drained and flaked, is another possibility. Even crumbled feta cheese or cubed pieces of Swiss or provolone cheese would complement this salad.

TABBOULEH

This salad, of Middle Eastern origin, is very simple and so refreshing, especially in the summer. Bulgur (cracked wheat, stocked at better supermarkets) is healthy and a delicious alternative to potatoes, rice, and pasta. Be forewarned if you taste this before it is refrigerated, it may seem flat or too "lemony." But you will be surprised what happens when the mixture has chilled. Trust us on this one.

1 cup bulgur
2 cups boiling water
1 cup minced fresh parsley

½ cup minced fresh mint
4 scallions with 3 to 4 inches of green part, thinly sliced
¼ cup freshly squeezed lemon juice
½ cup good-quality olive oil
Salt and freshly ground black pepper, to taste
4 ripe tomatoes, peeled (optional), seeded and diced
   (see below)

Place bulgur in a large bowl, pour boiling water over it, and allow to stand 1 hour. Drain thoroughly and return bulgur to bowl. Mix in parsley, mint, and scallions. Add lemon juice, olive oil, salt, and pepper. Cover and refrigerate 1 to 2 hours or until serving time.

Adjust seasonings after salad has chilled. If you find it too tart, you may add 1 to 2 tablespoons more olive oil and a little more salt. Add diced tomatoes just before serving and toss lightly to mix.
Serves 6 to 8.

Cook's Notes

- We often find great fresh parsley in the market at times, wash it, let it air dry, and then mince and freeze it in a covered container. It will keep for several months and is always available that way.

How to Peel and Seed Tomatoes

To peel, seed, and dice tomatoes: remove the peel by blanching in boiling water for 15 to 30 seconds before slipping the skin off. Alternatively, use a very sharp, swivel-action vegetable peeler to remove the skin without blanching. Cut the tomato in half horizontally, squeeze gently, and shake to remove most of the seeds and inner liquid. Then dice or chop with a sharp knife as directed in the recipe. It is not necessary to peel tomatoes, but if you wish to do so, follow the above directions.

THREE-BEAN SALAD

Our preference is very much for foods cooked from a fresh state, but once in a while we find the supermarket offers some great and tasty convenience. Such is the case with a bean salad made from three different varieties of canned beans. We recommend that you rinse all the beans in a colander before mixing them with the other ingredients. This helps remove a bit of the tinny taste that can be in the liquid. This is great picnic or barbecue fare.

Lemon Vinaigrette

⅓ cup extra-virgin olive oil

1 tablespoon freshly squeezed lemon juice

½ teaspoon Dijon-style mustard

1 clove garlic, peeled and finely chopped

½ teapsoon salt

Freshly ground black pepper, to taste

1 can (15 ounces) red kidney beans

1 can (15 ounces) white kidney beans or cannellini beans

1 can (15 ounces) chickpeas (garbanzo beans)

½ medium-size green bell pepper, seeded, deveined, and finely chopped

1 small red onion (about 4 ounces), thinly sliced

¼ cup chopped fresh parsley

3 slices bacon (optional), crisply cooked and chopped

Place the ingredients for vinaigrette in a glass jar with a tight-fitting lid. Shake well to mix and set aside.

Drain all the beans together in a colander. Rinse well and allow excess water to drain off. Place chopped bell pepper, sliced onion, and chopped parsley in a large mixing bowl. Add drained beans, pour on vinaigrette and mix well. Cover and refrigerate until ready to serve.

At serving time, place in a colorful bowl and, if you like, garnish with crisp bacon.
Serves 8.

Cook's Notes

- **This salad improves if made several hours to a day before serving.**
- **If you wish to make a smaller quantity of salad, just use two varieties of beans and then cut the other ingredients by a third.**
- **About ½ cup of any fresh and flavorful vinaigrette can be used to toss with the beans (see The Purist's Green Salad, page 40). A tablespoon of chopped fresh herbs also makes a nice addition, especially fresh basil or thyme.**

EGGS AND CHEESE

A bad rap revisited—foods too good to leave off your menu

HOW TO COOK AN EGG

It's simple. Most Americans like eggs. We like them fried, scrambled, poached (maybe perched atop a freshly browned nest of corned beef hash!), boiled, coddled, baked, in frittatas, and in omelets. Don't let the food police scare you into avoiding one of nature's finest foods. Build some balance into your eating habits and enjoy eggs as eggs now and then. Here are simple directions for the most common cooking methods: poaching, boiling, and frying.

Fried Eggs

For 1 to 3 eggs use a quality, preferably nonstick, 7- or 8-inch frying pan with a lid. Warm serving plates by running hot water over them and dry them. Heat pan over medium heat, adding 1 or 2 tablespoons unsalted butter or vegetable oil. When butter has melted or oil is hot crack eggs into pan, sprinkle very lightly with a pinch of salt and a quick grind of pepper, and cook until the whites have set. If you like your eggs "up" add a tablespoon of water to the pan when the whites start to set, and cover with a lid. The resulting steam will rapidly set the whites without overcooking the yolks. Turn the eggs, if you are serving them "over," using a thin spatula (see Cook's Notes, page 53, to learn how to flip eggs in the pan). Cook only a few seconds to firm the whites unless you like the yolks hard cooked. Slide the eggs onto a warmed plate.

< Omelet

Hard-Cooked Eggs

Use an egg piercer or clean sharp pin to poke a hole just through the shell on the large end of the egg. This allows the air bubble inside to get out without cracking the shell. To hard cook the egg, place it in a saucepan of cold water, bring the water to a boil, reduce to a simmer, and cook 12 minutes. If the egg is to be used cold later in, say, a salad, slip it into a medium bowl of cold water for a few minutes to help prevent the greenish ring around the yolk from developing. Remove shells just before using.

Soft-Cooked Eggs

Poke the shell as described above and slip the egg into a pan of boiling water. Reduce to a simmer and cook 3 or more minutes, depending on your preference. Rinse under cold water to make the eggs easier to handle and stop the cooking, and serve in shells immediately. You can buy little egg cups (usually porcelain) at kitchen shops to hold the egg neatly on a plate while you eat it, as well as little guillotines to nip the top off the shell!

Poached Eggs

Bring 2 inches of water and 1 teaspoon of vinegar or lemon juice to a simmer in a small, fairly shallow pan. Crack each egg into a separate small bowl and slip them (the eggs, not the bowls!) into the water. (Some kitchen shops carry a little metal cup with feet and a vertical wire handle which sits in the water and contains each egg in a perfect shape—crack eggs directly into these forms if using them.) Keep the water at a bare simmer, not a rolling boil. After 2 or 3 minutes, use a slotted spoon or the poaching form's wire handle to lift an egg to see whether the white has completely set. When it has, remove eggs with a slotted spoon and serve. If they are to be served cold later, slip them immediately into a medium bowl of cold water. They actually may be stored several days in the refrigerator in cold water—a good trick to know if poaching eggs for, say, eggs Benedict for a party.

SIMPLE (AND DELICIOUS) SCRAMBLED EGGS

The finest scrambled eggs are little more than a soft-cooked skillet custard. We normally think of them as breakfast food, but they make great, simple supper. Cook them to the firmness you desire, but do it slowly. We recommend serving them with Hash Browns (page 103) and perhaps some sliced fresh tomatoes drizzled with a little good-quality vinegar and olive oil.

> 5 large eggs
> Salt and freshly ground black pepper, to taste
> 1 tablespoon whipping cream or water
> 1/2 tablespoon unsalted butter

Heat a 10-inch nonstick skillet over medium heat for 2 minutes. In the meantime, beat eggs in a medium bowl with salt and pepper and cream or water. Add butter to the skillet and allow to melt. Swirl it around the pan and pour in eggs. Allow them to set for about 15 seconds and then begin to stir with a rubber spatula. Continue to stir slowly but consistently for

about 3 minutes, scraping the bottom of the skillet well with the spatula each time. The eggs should reach a medium-soft, custardy stage. Cook longer if you desire a firmer texture. Serve immediately on warm plates.
Serves 2.

Cook's Notes

- Add a tablespoon of chopped fresh chives or tarragon to the eggs just before they have set to the desired point. Ketchup is always a great accompaniment.

OMELET

Few stovetop skills can reward a humble cook with as much eating pleasure as the ability to make a decent omelet. A properly made omelet will be a little creamy in the center and perhaps lightly browned on the outside. It can be filled or plain, sauced or unsauced. The elegance is in the making, and making an omelet is easier than you might think. A slope-sided 8-inch frying pan is just right for a 3-egg omelet; use a 7-inch pan for a 2-egg version. Purists use seasoned steel or aluminum pans, but lots of us find it easier to use a nonstick pan. Gently warm serving plates just before making the omelet(s) by rinsing them with hot water, then drying with a towel.

> 3 large eggs, at room temperature
> Pinch salt and freshly ground pepper
> 2 tablespoons unsalted butter
> 1 tablespoon chopped fresh herbs (basil, tarragon, oregano, thyme, etc.)

In a small bowl, using a fork, beat eggs with salt and pepper until fluffy. Over medium-high heat melt butter in a frying pan. When butter has stopped foaming and before it burns, add eggs. Allow a few seconds for eggs to coagulate on the bottom, then use your fork to give eggs a quick stir. Allow a new "skin" to form on the bottom. Tilt the pan so that the omelet slides away from you toward the edge of the pan, and either push-jerk the pan (see Cook's Notes) so that the omelet folds over on itself or use a rubber spatula to fold it over. Allow to cook a few seconds to brown lightly, then turn or flip it over to brown lightly on the other side. When both sides are set and the center still feels soft—not firm or dry—slide your new-born omelet onto its plate and serve at once. Garnish with the fresh herb.

Serves 1.

Cook's Notes

◆ **The technique of "push-jerking" food in a slope-sided frying pan can make it easier to cook a great omelet, to flip fried eggs, and to toss vegetables while they sauté. Practice by putting a cup of dried beans or rice in your pan and repair to the back porch. Hold the pan level, push it away from you, and then jerk it just a little back toward you, raising the outside edge of the pan just slightly as you jerk. Sounds tough, but soon you'll be able to mix-toss your practice beans or rice without spilling much. That's the right time to apply for the egg-cooking job at the corner cafe!**

◆ **Variations are limitless. Add ½ cup of any filling you like, while the second skin is forming and before the omelet is folded. Try shredded cheese, cooked chopped potatoes, sautéed onions, sliced scallion tops, diced fresh tomatoes,** diced leftover bits of meat or shellfish. Just open the refrigerator door and use your imagination.

SWEET RED PEPPER AND POTATO FRITTATA

Frittatas are perfect ways to use up little bits of refrigerator odds and ends and still wind up with something rather elegant to eat. To make a frittata, one simply assembles an appealing mix of ingredients in a frying pan (preferably nonstick) and pours beaten eggs over those ingredients. A little heat from the stovetop, a little heat from the broiler, and good food happens!

> 2 russet potatoes (6 to 8 ounces each) or leftover potatoes
>   (see Cook's Notes)
> Salt, as needed
> ¼ cup olive oil
> 1 medium-size red or yellow onion (about 5 ounces), peeled and cut
>   into 1-inch dice, layers separated
> 1 red bell pepper, seeded, deveined, and cut into 1-inch dice
> 6 large eggs
> ¼ teaspoon hot pepper sauce
> Freshly ground black pepper, to taste
> ½ cup chopped fresh basil leaves
> 1 cup chopped fresh parsley leaves

Peel potatoes and cut into 1-inch dice. Place them in a 2-quart saucepan and cover with water. Bring to a boil, add 1 teaspoon salt, reduce to a simmer, and cook, partially covered, until potatoes are barely tender when pierced with a fork. Drain, immediately cover with cold water to stop the cooking, and allow to sit in the cold water about 3 minutes. Drain well.

Position an oven rack about 6 inches below the broiler element or flame and preheat broiler.

In a 10-inch frying pan with ovenproof handle, heat olive oil over medium-high heat. Add onion and bell pepper. Sauté, stirring occasionally, until vegetables have softened but are not wilted, about 3 minutes. While vegetables cook, crack the eggs into a medium bowl; using a fork, beat with pepper sauce, ½ teaspoon salt, pepper, basil, and parsley.

Reduce heat to medium, add potatoes, and cook several minutes until warmed through—try one. Turn heat down to medium low and pour egg mixture into pan. Cook without covering or stirring until egg mixture looks like it is about to set on top (it should quiver a little when you shake the pan.) Then place pan under broiler until frittata puffs a little and browns. Remove pan from broiler, let stand 1 or 2 minutes, and serve in wedges from the pan.
Serves 4.

Cook's Notes

◆ **Variations are unlimited. Simply remember to sauté raw foods before adding precooked foods, which just need warming. Frittatas are good at room temperature, too.**

◆ **If you have leftover cooked potatoes, peel them if you wish—you don't have to—and cut into 1-inch dice. Bring to room temperature before adding to the pan.**

◆ **Using a nonstick frying pan will make serving the frittata easier.**

SAVORY BREAD PUDDING

Known as "strata," this is one of our favorite brunch dishes, especially for company. You put it all together the night before, refrigerate it, and bake an hour or so before serving. You may want to make two for a large group because people will come back for seconds. Serve this dish with fresh fruit or juice and freshly baked bread and sweet rolls. Your guests will leave singing your praises. Strata means "layer," but has been attached to a casserole dish made with layered bread and other ingredients.

½ stick (4 tablespoons) unsalted butter, at room temperature

8 slices white or whole wheat bread, or a combination

8 ounces Cheddar cheese, shredded

1 can (15 ounces) diced mild green chilies

1 pound Black Forest ham (see Cook's Notes), cut into ½-inch cubes

8 eggs

3 cups milk

1 teaspoon salt

¼ teaspoon freshly ground black pepper

Butter a 9x13-inch baking dish. Butter bread slices and cut into 1-inch cubes. Place half the bread cubes in the bottom of the prepared baking dish. Sprinkle with half the cheese and chilies, then all the ham. Top with the remaining bread cubes, cheese, and chilies. Press down lightly with your hand.

In a large bowl, beat eggs with a whisk, then beat in milk, salt, and pepper to blend well and pour over the bread mixture. Cover tightly with plastic wrap and refrigerate overnight.

Next morning, about 1½ hours before you want to serve the casserole, preheat the oven to 350°F and remove the bread pudding from the refrigerator to warm it up slightly. Bake until pudding is set in the middle and doesn't appear runny when shaken gently, about 1 hour. Allow to stand for 10 to 15 minutes before serving.

Serves 8 to 12.

Cook's Notes

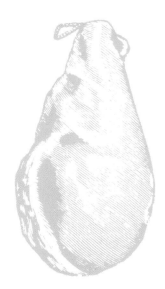

- **The number served depends on how you divide the dish. If you cut it in half lengthwise and crosswise into 4 sections, you will get 8 pieces. If you cut it lengthwise into 3 sections and crosswise into 4, it will yield 12 portions.**
- **You can halve this recipe and bake it in an 8-inch square baking dish to serve 4 to 6 as a family supper with a green salad.**
- **Here's an opportunity to use your pretty oven-to-table baking dishes, or a glass baking dish rather than aluminum.**
- **Black Forest ham is a gourmet ham that is cured with special seasonings in a German style. It is found in specialty markets and gourmet shops. If you can't find it, any good quality baked ham will do.**

A Primer on Cheese

Cheese is a wonderful food that has lately gotten a bum rap. The diet gurus are out to tell you not to eat cheese or to eat some tasteless stuff called low-fat cheese. Forget it, in our estimation. Once again we argue moderation. If fat and/or cholesterol are a problem, eat cheese less often or in moderate amounts, because there are few lunches or late suppers better than a couple of hunks of great cheese, good bread, and a nice bottle of wine.

In our recipes, we have highlighted cheeses from all over the world. In general we prefer buying cheese from the country of origin rather than the American version. A case in point is when Swiss is called for in a recipe, we prefer imported Emmenthaler to domestic Swiss-type cheeses. Now, don't get us wrong, American and Canadian cheese makers are doing some fantastic work. There is no better Cheddar than a good sharp one from Vermont, an aged Tillamook, or a Black Diamond from Canada, and, of course, California has given the world Monterey jack to cover all kinds of Tex-Mex goodies. Domestic ricotta and mozzarella are fine products also. We do encourage you to look for some of the fresh mozzarellas that are being done by specialty cheese makers. These soft cheeses are much more delicate and fresher tasting products than those found in sealed bags in the grocer's dairy case. Fetas and Muensters have good domestic and imported versions, but they vary in style, so taste around. But we really would encourage you to look for the imported versions when buying fontina, provolone, Gruyère, and Parmesan (which is sometimes shown as Parmigiana-Reggiano). Please, please, please do not buy pre-grated Parmesan in green cans.

Learn to choose your cheese purveyor as carefully as you choose your fish purveyor. Cheese is far less perishable than fish, but cheese does age, and if it looks brown and moldy, it likely is (although there are some cheeses meant to look this way, which is a subject for a longer dissertation). Many upscale supermarkets are beginning to show some very sophisticated cheese selections, but beware that their prices are sometimes higher than at the specialty cheese retailer. The grocery chains have to make a profit somewhere and they will do it on those items they don't have to highlight in discount ads.

Most cheese grates best when it's cold, with the exception of the very hard cheeses like Parmesan. But for just plain eating, all cheeses are better when they have been at room temperature for a couple of hours before serving.

Ham and Cheddar Quiche

OK, OK, you're going to read this recipe, see the words "whipping cream" and swear your doctor will never speak to you again. Just wait a moment, we are not asking you to cook this quiche every night, but when you do, make it right—light and fluffy and enriched with heavy cream, the way the French do it, and the way that made quiches so popular. Trust us, they did not become classics using skim milk!

Ham and Cheddar Quiche >

Pastry Crust, following

1 tablespoon unsalted butter

3 scallions with 1-inch green part, sliced into thin rings

1 cup finely diced Black Forest ham or other good-quality ham

3 large eggs

1½ cups whipping cream

Freshly ground black pepper, to taste

½ cup grated sharp Cheddar cheese (about 3 ounces)

Prepare and bake pastry crust. Preheat oven to 375°F.

Melt butter in a small frying pan over medium heat. When hot, add scallions and sauté until they are wilted. Add chopped ham and sauté until the edges have frizzled a little, about 2 minutes.

In a small bowl whisk together eggs, cream, and black pepper. Scatter the scallion-ham mixture over the bottom of the prebaked crust. Sprinkle grated Cheddar over this. Pour the egg mixture over it all, being careful not to go over the sides of the crust. Place immediately in oven and bake until slightly puffed and browned, 25 to 30 minutes. Allow to set 10 minutes before serving.

Serves 5.

Cook's Notes

◆ **The sky's the limit on variations here. Use all ham or all cheese, mixing the cheeses. Leftover cooked chicken or beef are wonderful. Just plan on 1½ to 2 cups of filling for this size quiche.**

Pastry Crust

We are repeating our recipe for this pastry crust from our first book, Entertaining People. It is the best we've found. But if pastry making still scares you, buy a prepared crust from the grocery store and make the quiche anyway. It will almost be as good. Then try crust making on a day when you are not rushed. It is really fun and the rewards are worth it.

2 cups all-purpose flour, plus more for rolling dough

½ teaspoon salt

1¼ sticks (5 ounces) very cold, unsalted butter, cut into
    ½-inch pieces

About ⅓ cup ice water

1 tablespoon Dijon-style mustard

Preheat oven to 400°F. Place flour and salt in the bowl of a food processor fitted with a steel blade. (See Cook's Notes for directions on making by hand.) Pulse once or twice to mix. Put in cold butter pieces and pulse several times until butter and flour are the texture of coarse meal. With the machine running slowly, add the ice water a bit at a time, stopping just before the dough forms a ball. (You may not need all the water.)

Place dough on a lightly floured surface and roll out with a rolling pin into a circle 11 inches in diameter. Transfer dough to a 9-inch cake pan with a removable bottom. Trim the edges so that they are even all the way around and the sides of the dough are about 1½ inches deep. Prick the bottom of the crust with a fork.

Place a piece of parchment paper or aluminum foil over the bottom of the crust and up the sides. Fill it with pie weights or dried beans or rice. Place the crust in the oven for 10 minutes. Then remove parchment or aluminum foil with its weights. Put crust back in the oven for another 10 minutes. Remove again from the oven and brush the bottom with mustard. Place crust back in the oven for 3 minutes; this will help seal the crust. Remove to a rack while making the filling.

Makes one 9-inch pie crust.

Cook's Notes

- **The directions for making the crust without a food processor are very much like making the biscuits for Strawberry Shortcake (page 155). Place dry ingredients in a large mixing bowl. Divide butter into about 10 pieces and then work it into the flour with your fingertips. Blend ice water in with a fork just until the dough holds together; then turn it out on a floured surface. Knead a couple of times and then form into a disk. Proceed to roll out as directed.**
- **When transferring the pastry dough to the baking pan, roll it up jelly-roll style over the rolling pin. Position it at the edge of the pan and begin to unroll, adjusting its position. This causes less tearing of the crust.**
- **Save the trimmings of the raw dough. If there are tears in the crust or shrinkage in the oven, you can easily patch.**
- **The dough can be made in advance, rolled out, placed in the pan, and frozen, well wrapped, for 1 month. It bakes beautifully from a frozen state. This works so well, you might think about doubling the recipe and having one unbaked crust available in the freezer.**

- **If using the crust for a sweet tart, brush it with beaten egg yolk instead of mustard.**
- **If you wish, you can use a removable-bottom quiche pan, which is available from a kitchenware store. The edges of this type of pan are fluted and make an attractive crust.**

CHEESE PIE

Every cook needs a few utterly simple, yet satisfying, recipes. This is one of those. If you can stir and grate some cheese, you can make this recipe. We serve this for a light dinner, accompanied with a salad. Alternatively, it could be used as part of a brunch. Young children, even picky ones, like this Cheese Pie. Cooked in a pie plate or 10-inch ovenproof skillet, the pie puffs up, browns lightly on top, and has crispy edges.

Butter, for greasing pan
1 extra-large egg
$3/4$ cup all-purpose flour
$1/2$ teaspoon salt
$1/2$ teaspoon freshly ground black pepper
1 cup milk
1 cup grated Muenster cheese (about 4 ounces)

Preheat oven to 425°F. Butter a 9-inch glass pie plate or 10-inch ovenproof skillet. In a medium bowl, beat egg. Add flour, salt, pepper, and $1/2$ cup of the milk. Stir until smooth, then add remaining $1/2$ cup milk and stir to combine. Add cheese, stir to combine, then pour into prepared pan. Bake until puffed and nicely browned, 25 to 30 minutes. Cut into wedges and serve immediately.

Serves 3 to 4.

Cook's Notes

◆ **If you have a 9-inch cast iron skillet, bake the Cheese Pie in it. The bottom and sides of the pie get wonderfully crispy.**

◆ **Cheese Pie is best when eaten right from the oven. However, leftovers rewarm well in a 400°F oven.**

◆ **Try other cheeses. Half Cheddar and half Muenster works well. Fontina or Gruyère are also possibilities. We find Swiss cheese makes the pie too stringy and gooey.**

◆ **Several slices of cooked bacon can be crumbled and added to the batter.**

CHEESE FONDUE

It is nice when a fad becomes a classic, or in this case, when a classic becomes a fad and then returns to its rightful place in the culinary world. Anyone who has been to Switzerland knows that fondue has always been an integral part of its cuisine. The Swiss know, and now you can, what a wonderful meal this is on a cold winter's night, or what a pleasing part of a buffet selection.

1 loaf French bread (about 1 pound), cut into ¹/₂-inch cubes

1¹/₂ cups dry white wine

1 pound shredded mild cheese (our favorite combination is half imported Swiss Emmenthaler and half imported Gruyère)

3 tablespoons all-purpose flour

Preheat oven to 325°F. Spread out bread cubes in a baking sheet and bake until bread feels crisp on the outside but slightly soft within, 20 to 25 minutes.

Warm wine in a saucepan over low heat. Toss shredded cheese with flour in a large mixing bowl. When steam begins to rise from wine, slowly add cheese, a handful at a time, while stirring with a wooden spoon. Allow each handful to melt a bit before stirring in more.

When all the cheese has been added to the pan and heated through, test for consistency. The fondue should coat a piece of bread nicely, but not be too thick. Add a little more wine, if necessary, to thin.

Warm your fondue pot by filling it with hot tap water and letting it sit for a couple of minutes. Drain the water and dry the pot. Pour in the hot cheese mixture. Place bread cubes in a large deep bowl. Provide guests with small plates and long-handled fondue forks for dipping the bread cubes in the cheese.

Serves 4 as main course, 8 as appetizer.

Cook's Notes

- If your fondue pot has not been warmed before adding the melted cheese, the cheese will firm up and you will need to remelt it.

- If your fondue pot is made of metal, melt the fondue directly in it and save the extra cleanup.

- A whisk can be very handy for the final mixing of cheese into wine.

- Don't hesitate to try other blends of cheeses. Hard cheeses are best and Cheddar always tastes great. You can also use a firm whole wheat bread instead of French bread for the cubes.

- Don't fret if you don't have an official fondue pot. No worry, just use a heavyweight saucepan, 2- to $2\frac{1}{2}$-quart capacity.

PASTA, BEANS, AND GRAINS

Carbohydrates in the spotlight—plus plenty of meatless protein

UNDERSTANDING AND COOKING
FRESH AND DRIED PASTA

Everybody loves pasta and, if ever there was a politically correct food for the nineties, this is it! Cooking pasta is easy. It is healthy (at least, if the sauce isn't too rich). And it can be dressed up for company or dressed down for a quick family meal.

At the supermarket today, you are going to be presented with two types of pasta—fresh and dried. We like them both and feel that each has its place.

Fresh pastas are found generally in the refrigerated or deli section of your supermarket. They are sometimes frozen, but then must be cooked from a frozen state. (Defrosting first will turn fresh pasta into one solid mass of dough.) Fresh pasta is excellent with light, delicate sauces, for example, our Olive Oil, Garlic, and Herbs (page 68). Fresh pasta cooks *very* quickly, literally in 1 to 2 minutes in boiling water.

Dried pastas are best with hearty, meaty sauces—like those Mom used to make. Dried pasta does take a bit longer to cook than fresh, but it is still a candidate for the "quick-cook" approach to dinner. Package directions for dried pasta generally call for 6 to 14 minutes of cooking time depending on the size of the noodle. We frequently find these times a bit too long for our taste, and in a moment we will discuss how to determine doneness.

Whether using fresh or dried pasta, always start with plenty of water. We recommend 8 quarts to cook 1 pound of pasta. Pasta water should always be salted, but we recommend you do so after it comes to a boil. Unsalted water boils more quickly than salted water and you are not as likely to corrode your fine pots. Many recipes will recommend adding 1 or 2 tablespoons olive oil to the pasta pot. There is certainly no harm in this but we have not seen it make much difference.

We now need to discuss that all-important Italian pasta cooking term, *al dente*. This means literally "to the tooth," or, in other words: Cook the pasta until tender but still firm to the bite, not mushy. We feel that there is only one way to truly test if the pasta is done: Pull a piece out of the water with tongs or a fork and taste it. You may have heard of the idea of throwing a piece of spaghetti against the wall to see if it sticks (the thought being that if it does, the pasta is done). You are welcome to try it, but please don't ask us to recommend house painters.

Drain your pasta in a colander that is large enough to hold it all, so it doesn't slide out into the sink. Rinse only if you are not going to sauce and serve it immediately. If using pasta later or in a pasta salad, rinse well and then toss with 1 or 2 tablespoons vegetable oil or olive oil to keep it from sticking.

<   Linguine with Olive Oil, Garlic, and Herbs

Spaghetti with Cooked Tomato Sauce

The sauce for this spaghetti is our favorite recipe for a basic, very adaptable tomato sauce. Make the sauce ahead, if you like; double the recipe and freeze in smaller quantities; or cut the recipe in half and have a smaller quantity that will serve four for dinner. We use this tomato sauce in our recipe for lasagna and it also works well as a sauce for tortellini, ravioli, or just about any pasta. We always have some in our freezers at home for an easy, last-minute dinner.

3 cups Cooked Tomato Sauce, following
1 pound good-quality dried spaghetti
Salt, for cooking pasta
Freshly grated Parmesan cheese

Prepare tomato sauce and keep warm. Cook spaghetti as directed on page 65. After draining, divide among individual warm plates or place all in a pasta bowl. Top with sauce and serve with freshly grated Parmesan cheese.
Serves 4.

Cooked Tomato Sauce

$1/4$ cup olive oil
1 large yellow onion (about 12 ounces), peeled and diced
3 large cloves garlic, peeled and minced
2 carrots, diced
2 ribs celery, tops removed and diced
2 cans (28 ounces each) Italian-style peeled tomatoes, drained, reserving liquid, and chopped

1 bay leaf
2 teaspoons dried oregano
2 teaspoons dried basil
1 teaspoon salt
1 teaspoon granulated sugar
$1/2$ teaspoon freshly ground black pepper
$1/3$ cup minced fresh parsley

In a 4-quart non-aluminum saucepan, heat oil over medium-high heat until hot. Add onion, garlic, carrots, and celery to pan. Cook and stir until vegetables are well coated with oil. Reduce heat to medium, cover pan, and cook until vegetables are tender, about 10 minutes. Add tomatoes, reserved liquid, bay leaf, oregano, basil, salt, sugar, and pepper. Stir to combine and let sauce simmer, uncovered, until the liquid has cooked down and the sauce is thick, about 30 minutes. Add minced parsley and simmer an additional 10 minutes. Remove from heat. If you like a chunky sauce, then the sauce is ready to serve. Otherwise, use a food processor or blender and purée the sauce in batches. Return to the pan and keep warm while you cook the pasta.
Makes about 7 cups.

Tomato Sauce with Meat

As a variation to the basic Tomato Sauce, sauté $3/4$ pound of ground beef or bulk Italian sausage, drain off the fat, then add to the sauce for a meat tomato sauce. Make meatballs using a combination of ground beef and ground pork, adding a little salt and freshly ground black pepper. Brown and cook separately, then add to the sauce.

Cook's Notes

- If fresh herbs are available, use them. Substitute 2 tablespoons freshly minced basil and 2 tablespoons freshly minced oregano for the dried basil and oregano. Add the fresh herbs with the parsley for the last 10 minutes of cooking.
- When tomatoes are at their best in late summer, substitute 4 pounds fresh tomatoes for the canned in the recipe. Peel, seed, and chop the tomatoes (page 46), reserving as much of the juice as possible.
- Allow about ¼ pound uncooked spaghetti and ¾ cup cooked tomato sauce per person.
- This sauce is so versatile it can also be used with fish. Buy fresh halibut steaks or red snapper fillets, place in a shallow baking dish, then spoon enough tomato sauce over the fish to cover. Bake in a preheated 375°F oven until the fish flakes when tested with a fork, about 25 minutes.

ROTINI WITH FRESH TOMATO SAUCE

This is quick cooking at its finest and, we might add, very healthy. If rotini isn't available, use corkscrew noodles, bow-ties, or large macaroni.

Fresh Tomato Sauce, following
1½ pounds dried rotini pasta or other spiral noodle
Olive oil, for cooked pasta

Prepare tomato sauce. Cook pasta as directed on page 65. After draining, toss pasta with a little olive oil (just enough to coat it). Divide pasta among individual, warmed bowls. Top with the room temperature sauce and serve immediately. *Serves 6.*

Fresh Tomato Sauce

This is a simple and delicious uncooked sauce suitable for the late summer or early fall when tomatoes are full of ripe, sweet flavor. It can be made at the last minute, as well as a couple of hours ahead of serving. It then gets a little juicier and gives the flavors a bit of time to blend. We especially like this on spiraled pasta, but it's great on any noodle.

2½ pounds vine-ripened tomatoes, peeled, seeded, and coarsely chopped (page 46)
2 shallots, peeled and minced
1 small clove garlic, peeled and minced
1 cup coarsely chopped fresh basil
⅓ cup coarsely chopped fresh parsley (preferably Italian flat-leaf)
¼ cup extra-virgin olive oil
2 tablespoons balsamic vinegar
1 teaspoon salt
Freshly ground black pepper, to taste

Combine all ingredients in a large mixing bowl. Set aside at room temperature until ready to use, up to 3 hours.
Makes about 4 cups.

Cook's Notes

- Basil is certainly a natural with tomatoes, but other fresh herbs work very well, particularly fresh tarragon or fresh mint.

LINGUINE WITH OLIVE OIL, GARLIC, AND HERBS

Here is a very simple pasta dish that is both delicious and healthy. It makes an excellent accompaniment to meat or it can be served with a salad as a meatless main dish. This recipe illustrates that the finest and freshest ingredients can make a seemingly simple offering as superb as the most complicated dish.

1/4 cup good-quality olive oil

3 cloves garlic, peeled and finely minced

1 teaspoon salt

1 pound fresh or dried linguine

1/2 cup chopped fresh herbs (parsley, basil, or a mixture)

1/4 teaspoon freshly ground black pepper

1/2 cup freshly grated Parmesan cheese

Fill an 8- to 10-quart stockpot 3/4 full with water and bring to a boil. The water will heat faster—about 10 minutes—if you cover the pot.

Heat olive oil in an 8-inch frying pan over medium heat for 1 minute. Add minced garlic and cook, stirring, until garlic begins to turn light brown, 1 to 2 minutes. (Watch carefully for the color change, because overcooked garlic has an unpleasant taste.) Remove pan from heat and set aside.

Add salt to the stockpot when the water comes to a boil. Now add linguine and cook until *al dente* as directed on page 65. Fresh pasta should be done about 30 seconds after the

water boils again; dried pasta will take about 10 minutes. Drain pasta immediately in a colander, but do not rinse the pasta.

Return the drained linguine to the stockpot and add the garlic-oil mixture. Stir to coat pasta well. Cook for 1 or 2 minutes over low heat. (This cooks away any water that has clung to the pasta.) Sprinkle herbs and black pepper over pasta and toss lightly. Place pasta in a warm serving bowl and serve immediately. Pass the Parmesan to be sprinkled on top of the pasta.

Serves 4 to 6.

LASAGNA

An all-time favorite, lasagna is a perfect do-ahead entrée. Families and friends enjoy the simplicity of pasta, a good salad, good bread, and a light dessert. Our poached pears, baked apples, or even a fruit cobbler would be a perfect finish to this meal. When made just for our families, we enjoy the leftovers another night.

3 cups Cooked Tomato Sauce (page 66)

10 strips dried lasagna noodles (see Cook's Notes)

1 pound bulk Italian sausage

2 tablespoons olive oil

1 cup minced fresh parsley

1 pound part-skim ricotta cheese

8 ounces whole-milk mozzarella cheese, shredded

4 ounces Parmesan cheese, freshly grated (about 1 cup)

Prepare tomato sauce and keep warm. Cook lasagna noodles in boiling water in an 8-quart stockpot as directed on page 65. Drain, rinse with cold water, and reserve.

Heat a 10-inch frying pan over medium-high heat. Add Italian sausage and sauté until meat is no longer pink. Drain excess fat and reserve sausage.

Brush the bottom and sides of a 9x13-inch baking dish with olive oil. Lay 3 strips of lasagna noodles lengthwise in the bottom of prepared dish. Add 1½ cups of the tomato sauce and spread evenly. Scatter the sausage evenly over the sauce. Now scatter ½ cup of the parsley on top. Start the second layer by placing 3 more sheets of lasagna in the pan. Use a rubber spatula to spread all the ricotta evenly over the pasta. Cover ricotta with remaining 1½ cups tomato sauce. Sprinkle remaining ½ cup parsley on top. Now scatter all the mozzarella evenly on top. Add 3 more sheets of lasagna for the final layer. Cover the pasta with all of the Parmesan. At this point, cover and refrigerate the lasagna to bake later or cover tightly with plastic wrap and freeze.

About an 1¼ hours before serving, preheat oven to 350°F. Bake lasagna until it is lightly browned at the edges and bubbly, 45 to 50 minutes. Let rest for 10 minutes before cutting into squares. If baking from a frozen state, start in a cold oven (especially if your pan is porcelain or glass) and allow about 20 to 30 extra minutes of baking time.
Serves 8 to 10.

Cook's Notes

- If you are calorie conscious, substitute part-skim mozzarella and low-fat ricotta.

- You will probably need to buy a 1-pound box of lasagna; reserve extra noodles for another use. Although the recipe only requires 9 strips of noodles, we always cook an extra one in case of breakage.

- If a pasta store in your area carries sheets of fresh pasta, substitute 3 sheets (¾ pound) for the dried called for in the recipe. With fresh pasta, just lightly rinse the sheets of any flour that keeps them from sticking together and use them without precooking. Fresh pasta is a wonderful time saver here.

- Use spinach pasta instead of egg pasta, if you prefer.

- If you prefer a meatless lasagna, skip the Italian sausage. You might substitute sliced artichoke hearts for the sausage; use an 8-ounce jar, drain, pat dry, and slice the artichokes.

- Another alternative for a meatless lasagna is to use thin slices of eggplant. Slice 1 small eggplant lengthwise, brush slices with olive oil, and sauté in a 12-inch frying pan until nicely browned on both sides. Place eggplant slices instead of sausage over sauce in the first layer.

Three-Bean Meatless Chili

You can make this chili as hot or mild as you prefer simply by increasing the amount of jalapeño or using mild green chilies instead. This recipe makes a large pot of chili, but it freezes and reheats very well for a quick supper later. We like it served over steamed basmati rice or small pasta such as elbow macaroni.

Chili Seasonings

$1\frac{1}{2}$ tablespoons brown sugar

$2\frac{1}{2}$ tablespoons ground cumin

3 tablespoons chili powder

$\frac{1}{8}$ teaspoon ground cloves

$\frac{1}{8}$ teaspoon ground allspice

3 teaspoons dried oregano

2 tablespoons olive oil

1 large or 2 medium-size yellow onions (about 10 ounces total), peeled and chopped

4 cloves garlic, peeled and minced

1 green bell pepper, seeded, deveined, and finely chopped

1 fresh jalapeño chili, seeded and finely chopped

1 can (15 ounces) diced green chilies

1 can (28 ounces) peeled, chopped tomatoes with liquid

1 can (15 ounces) tomato sauce

2 cans (15 ounces each) black beans, drained

1 can (15 ounces) pinto beans, drained

1 can (15 ounces) cannellini or white kidney beans, drained

3 tablespoons chopped fresh cilantro

In a small bowl, mix together chili seasonings and set aside. In a heavy 6-quart saucepan or stockpot, heat oil over medium heat and sauté onions, garlic, bell peppers, jalapeño, and green chilies until onions are translucent, about 5 minutes. Add tomatoes, tomato sauce, and reserved chili seasonings. Reduce heat and simmer, uncovered, for 15 minutes. Add beans and simmer 20 minutes more. If the mixture becomes too thick, add water, about $\frac{1}{4}$ cup at a time, but don't let chili get watery. Garnish with cilantro and serve.
Serves 8.

Chili con Carne

After heating oil, sauté 1 pound very lean ground beef until it loses its red color. Add onions, garlic, and peppers and continue as above, using only 1 can of black beans instead of 2.

Cook's Notes

- **When cleaning jalapeños, do not rub your eyes or face with your hands until you are finished and have washed them with soap and water. Otherwise you could get an unpleasant surprise—a burn.**

Bean Burritos

Like Red Beans and Rice, this is an example of "peasant food" that nearly everyone loves to eat! (We don't know who coined that phrase,

Bean Burrito >

but it is descriptive.) Inexpensive, filling, and loaded with intense flavor, these bean burritos are easy to prepare and assemble, especially if you cook the beans a day or two in advance.

1 cup dried pinto beans, small red beans, black beans, or kidney beans

Bean Seasonings

1 large clove garlic, peeled and sliced

1 whole scallion, including green top, sliced

1 teaspoon ground cumin

$1/2$ teaspoon dried oregano

$1/8$ teaspoon crushed red pepper

Freshly ground black pepper, to taste

1 slice bacon, cut into small dice

1 tablespoon chopped fresh cilantro

Salt to taste (about $1^1/2$ teaspoons)

4 large flour tortillas, 9 to 10 inches in diameter

4 scallions, white part chopped and green part thinly sliced,
    reserve separately

8 ounces sharp Cheddar cheese, shredded

$1/2$ cup chopped fresh cilantro

$3/4$ cup sour cream

1 jar good-quality mild or hot salsa

Wash and pick over beans, removing any stones or debris. Place them in a 2-quart saucepan and add 4 cups cold water. Bring to a boil, cover, turn off heat, and allow beans to soak for 1 hour. Drain beans, cover with 3 cups water, bring to a boil, and boil 10 minutes, uncovered. Add bean seasonings except salt, reduce to a simmer, cover, and cook until the beans are tender but not mushy, 20 to 30 minutes. Stir in the salt.

Place a tortilla on each of 4 warmed plates. Using a slotted spoon, so that the beans are well drained, portion $1/4$ of the beans onto one side of each tortilla. Scatter chopped white part of scallions, cheese, and cilantro over the beans, and fold over tortilla to cover bean mixture. Top with a little sour cream and garnish with sliced scallion tops. Serve with salsa on the side. Serves 4.

Cook's Notes

◆ **Substitute plain yogurt for the sour cream; use mild jack cheese in place of Cheddar; top with a canned enchilada sauce; garnish with sliced black olives; add thinly sliced or diced leftover meat or poultry to the bean filling.**

◆ **For a vegetarian burrito leave out the bacon when cooking the beans, and include some white or brown cooked rice as filling.**

RED BEANS AND RICE

This is a fine example of why even rich people love peasant food! So beloved in the American South, Red Beans and Rice costs little to make but tastes so good that it is hard to push oneself away from the table. Use of the quick-soak method of softening dried beans allows this dish to be prepared in about two hours. Most of that time the pot will be simmering quietly on the stovetop, requiring little attention from you. Beans and rice served together happen to be highly nutritious, a happy circumstance if payday is a week away but your wallet is almost empty!

½ pound dried small red beans

4 scallions

1 smoked pork shank or hock (about 1 pound)

1 small yellow onion (about 3 ounces), peeled and cut into
    1-inch pieces

2 cloves garlic, peeled

½ rib celery, sliced, or ¼ teaspoon celery seed

1 bay leaf

¼ teaspoon crushed red pepper flakes

½ teaspoon dried thyme

Freshly ground black pepper, to taste

2 cups long-grain white rice

Salt to taste, if necessary

Wash and pick over beans, removing any stones or debris. Place them in a 3-quart saucepan and add 4 cups cold water. Bring to a boil, cover, turn off heat, and allow beans to soak for 1 hour.

Drain the soaking liquid and add 4 cups cold water to the beans. Bring them to a boil and boil, uncovered, for 10 full minutes. Slice white part of scallions and about 2 inches of green part and add to beans. Slice remaining green tops of scallions and reserve for garnish. Then add to beans the smoked pork, onion, garlic, celery, bay leaf, red pepper flakes, thyme, and black pepper. Bring pot back to a boil, reduce to a simmer, and cook, partly covered, until beans are tender but not mushy, 30 to 40 minutes. Meanwhile cook rice as directed on page 75.

Remove smoked pork and let cool enough to handle. Pick the smoked pork off the bone, discarding skin and bone. Cut meat into ¼-inch pieces and return them to the bean pot. Taste beans for salt—the salty smoked pork may have seasoned them quite enough.

To serve, portion a cup of freshly cooked white rice into a large individual soup or pasta bowl for each person. Ladle 1 to 1½ cups beans around the edge of the bowl, leaving rice visible in the middle. Garnish each bowl with the reserved sliced scallion tops and serve hot.

Serves 6.

Cook's Notes

◆   **You may substitute kidney beans, pinto beans, or black beans; the color of the finished dish may vary a little, but the flavor will be just as good.**

LENTILS AND RICE

Middle Eastern and Asian cooking have many delicious meatless dishes, which, in light of today's imperative to eat healthier, are certainly worth trying. Lentils and rice, flavored with onions and a blend of spices, is one of our favorites. Served with a dollop of low-fat or non-fat plain yogurt and a tossed green salad, this makes a well-balanced vegetarian meal. Lentils and rice can also be served as a side dish with grilled meat, if you like.

Spice Mixture

1 teaspoon freshly ground black pepper

½ teaspoon ground coriander

½ teaspoon ground cloves

1 teaspoon ground cumin

⅛ teaspoon ground cardamom

⅛ teaspoon ground nutmeg

Pinch ground cinnamon

4 cups water

1 cup lentils, washed and drained

1 cup converted rice (see Cook's Notes)

¼ cup olive oil

2 medium-size yellow onions (about 5 ounces each),
   peeled and thinly sliced

2 teaspoons salt

1 cup plain yogurt (optional)

Combine spice mixture in a small bowl and set aside.

Bring the water to a boil in a 6-quart saucepan. Add lentils
and cook, uncovered, over medium heat for 15 minutes.
Add rice, bring to a boil again, reduce heat to low, cover,
and simmer until the liquid is absorbed, 20 to 25 minutes.
Set aside, covered, to steam until ready to serve.

Just before serving, heat olive oil over medium heat in a
10-inch frying pan and add onions. Sauté until onions start
to turn brown and just begin to "burn" around the edges,
about 15 minutes. Add reserved spice mixture and salt to
onions and sauté an additional minute. Put lentil and rice
mixture in serving bowl, add onion-spice mixture, and toss
to mix thoroughly. Serve immediately. Pass a bowl of yogurt,
if you like, for a topping.

Serves 4 to 6 as a main course, 6 to 8 as a side dish.

Cook's Notes

◆   **In this instance, converted rice (packaged parboiled rice) is
the best choice because it stays firm and will not become
mushy and overcooked.**

A GUIDE TO RICE

Most beginning cooks and lots of experienced cooks don't
understand very much about rice. There are several varieties
of rice on the market and each requires a different cooking
time and proportion of water to rice. Chinese-style "sticky"
rice is based on a different grain and different cooking
method than, say, Western-style long-grain "fluffy" rice.
Listed here are the most popular rices available in America
along with a brief description of their attributes.

Arborio rice. A short-grain Italian rice. It can be cooked
for a long time and can absorb much liquid and still remain
firm and creamy. Used in the classic Italian rice dish, risotto.

Basmati rice. A thin, long-grain rice, which is grown in
India and surrounding areas. It has a nutty flavor and can be
used in almost any rice dish. Some is now grown in Texas
and called "Texmati."

Brown rice. This is rice in its most natural form, with the
bran layer still attached. It has a stronger, nutty flavor than
white rice and takes twice as long to cook. There are several

new "quick cooking" brown rices available, but they are not as flavorful because they have been precooked.

Long-grain white rice. A long rice with tapered ends. When it is cooked, it is fluffy and separated. Used in pilafs, curries, rice salads, and rice puddings.

Short-grain or medium-grain white rice. Medium-grain rice is slightly rounded and short-grain is very rounded. Used in Asian cooking and sometimes called pearl rice. The shorter the grain, the stickier the rice.

Wild rice. This is not really a rice, but the seed of a water grass that grows in the region of the Great Lakes. It is expensive and takes a very long time to cook. Wild rice is often mixed with long-grain rice after they have been cooked separately.

Converted rice. This rice has been presteamed or par-boiled. Since it is less sticky than natural rice, we sometimes use it in dishes where we want firm, separate grains.

Instant rice. This is a precooked rice that is then freeze-dried. It has a very bland flavor. We don't recommend it.

BASIC METHOD FOR COOKING WHITE RICE

*Some people fear riding in elevators. Others are afraid to walk under ladders. And, sadly, thousands (probably millions) of Americans face each new day fearing that they might be asked to produce an accept-*able batch of cooked rice! Rice cookery seems an alien experience for many of us, so here is a simple method for cooking long- or short-grain white rice, the two most commonly used varieties. What matters is learning the basic proportions of water to rice. Once you've mastered these proportions, you may expect fine results regardless of how little or how much rice you are cooking. An important step in our method for cooking rice is to "wash" the rice first. Some package directions don't include this step or even tell you it is not necessary; we disagree. Typically, rice is preserved by being coated with rice flour. By washing the rice you are merely removing this coating and other unwelcome objects like pebbles and husks.*

Long-Grain Rice

   1 or more cups long-grain white rice

   2 cups water for first cup uncooked rice, plus

      $1\frac{1}{2}$ cups water for each additional cup rice

   $\frac{1}{2}$ teaspoon salt for each cup uncooked rice

Short-Grain Rice

   1 or more cups short- or medium-grain white rice

   $1\frac{1}{2}$ cups water for first cup uncooked rice, plus

      1 cup water for each additional cup rice

   $\frac{1}{2}$ teaspoon salt for each cup uncooked rice

Use a pot that is at least double the water volume you are planning to use. (For example, a 2-quart saucepan is fine when using 2 cups uncooked rice and 4 cups water.) Place rice in pan and add water to cover rice. Use your hand to "wash" the rice by swishing it around in the water. Drain the water. Repeat this washing until the water runs clear, usually 2 additional times. Drain well.

Add the measured water to rice and the appropriate amount of salt. Bring to a boil over high heat, cover pan, turn heat to low, and let the rice cook for an additional 15 minutes (don't peek!). Remove from heat and let the rice sit until you are ready to serve. (If you have a gas stove, turning down the flame is all you need do after water comes to a boil. But if you have an electric stove, you should set another burner to low and move the pot once the water has come to a boil; otherwise you risk the water boiling over.)

1 cup uncooked rice yields 3 cups cooked rice, serves 3 or 4.

Cook's Notes

- **Cooked rice can be served plain, assuming that whatever you are serving it with has a sauce. For example, serve rice with a curried dish or a braised dish, such as Braised Lamb Shanks.**

- **Add some butter and freshly minced parsley to the cooked rice. This makes a nice accompaniment to poached chicken breasts or sautéed fish.**

- **Leftovers? Rice reheats well. The easiest way is to cover it and heat it in the microwave. Reheating it in the oven is also an option. To do that, place the rice in an ovenproof dish, sprinkle a little bit of water over the rice, cover it with aluminum foil, and bake in a preheated 300°F oven for about 20 minutes.**

- **Rice pancakes anyone? Mix the cold rice with beaten eggs (this mixture should be light, but not runny). Add a touch of salt and cook as if you were making pancakes. With a little butter and maple syrup this makes a fine breakfast!**

BROWN RICE, PILAF STYLE

To be honest, not one of us has ever particularly liked steamed brown rice because its texture always seemed mushy. But brown rice is a healthy, high-fiber type of rice because the bran layer is still attached. Thus we felt compelled to develop a recipe that would make the rice more texturally interesting. Borrowing from the method in which pilaf is cooked, we tried sautéing the rice in oil before adding water. Voila! Brown rice with good texture and taste.

    1 cup brown rice
    2 tablespoons olive oil
    2¼ cups water, for cooking
    Pinch salt

Place rice in medium bowl and add enough water to cover rice. Use your hand to "wash" the rice by swishing it around in the water. Drain water. Repeat this washing until the water runs clear, usually 2 additional times. Drain well and set aside.

Heat a heavy 2½-quart saucepan over medium-high heat. When hot, add oil. Tilt pan to spread oil, then add the washed rice. Sauté, stirring constantly, until rice is well coated with oil, about 3 minutes. Add the 2¼ cups water and salt to pan, and bring to a boil over high heat. Cover pot, reduce heat to low, and let the rice cook for 45 minutes. Remove from heat and let stand, covered, for 10 minutes longer. Serve immediately or keep warm until ready to serve.

Fluff with a fork before serving.

Makes 3 cups cooked rice, serves 3 or 4.

Variation with onion. Use an additional tablespoon of oil and sauté ¹/₂ cup finely chopped yellow onion for 3 minutes before adding the rice. See Basmati Rice Pilaf Cook's Notes for additional seasoning suggestions.

Cook's Notes

- **To increase quantities follow these proportions: Use 2¼ cups water for the first cup of dry rice, then add 1¾ cups water for each additional cup of rice.**
- **You will see both short- and long-grain brown rice on the grocer's shelf; we prefer the long grain, but decide for yourself.**
- **Use chicken, beef, or vegetable stock instead of water in the recipe.**

BASMATI RICE PILAF

What makes basmati rice unique, whether grown in India or Texas, is its wonderfully nutty flavor. In this recipe the technique of first sautéing the rice in oil keeps the grains separate and firm. The result is a rice dish that becomes a focal point of a meal. Pilaf served with a small portion of grilled lamb, chicken, or beef and a grilled or sautéed vegetable makes a delightful summer meal. Our recipe for Curried Chicken or Turkey would also be enhanced with a side serving of rice pilaf. Leftover pilaf reheats well in a microwave or can even be frozen.

2 cups basmati rice

3 tablespoons vegetable oil

1 large yellow onion (about 8 ounces), peeled and finely chopped

1 tablespoon minced fresh ginger root

2 teaspoons salt

2 teaspoons ground cumin

2 teaspoons ground coriander

3 cups Chicken Stock (page 32) or canned low-sodium chicken broth

Preheat oven to 325°F. Place rice in a medium bowl, cover with cold water, swish rice around with your hand, and drain water. Repeat 2 more times. On the final washing, drain rice very well and set aside.

Heat a 3-quart straight-sided frying pan with ovenproof handles over medium-high heat. When hot, add oil. Tilt pan to spread oil, then add onion and ginger. Sauté, stirring frequently, until onion is soft, about 5 minutes (lower heat if ginger is beginning to burn). Add salt, cumin, and coriander; sauté, stirring constantly, 1 minute longer. Add rice to pan, sauté, stirring constantly, until rice is coated with oil and turns whitish, 2 to 3 minutes. Add stock, turn heat to high, and cook uncovered until all the stock on the surface of the rice disappears and small holes form, about 5 minutes. Cover pan with a tight-fitting lid and place in preheated oven for 20 minutes. Taste the rice; it should be tender, but still slightly firm. Bake longer if needed.

Serve immediately, or keep warm until ready to serve. The rice reheats well, either covered in the microwave or in a 300°F oven.

Serves 6 to 8.

Cook's Notes

- If you want to make half the recipe to serve just a few, cut all ingredients in half except the stock. Use 2 cups chicken stock for 1 cup of rice.
- Well-stocked grocery stores are carrying basmati rice. This type of rice produced in Texas is called "Texmati" rice. Look for this rice under either name.
- The combination of fresh ginger and spices given for this pilaf recipe lend themselves well to grilled foods or other foods done in a Middle Eastern or Indian style. If you want a pilaf to accompany Lamb Shanks (page 141), or Roast Loin of Pork (page 138), substitute 1 teaspoon of garlic for the fresh ginger, and use thyme and crushed rosemary instead of cumin and coriander. Or, substitute Italian herbs such as basil and oregano.
- Once the rice is cooked, stir in sautéed pine nuts, or cooked peas, or other diced cooked vegetables.
- Plump ¼ cup raisins, golden raisins, or currants in 2 tablespoons warm water for 10 minutes. Add to recipe when you add the stock.

RISOTTO WITH TOMATOES AND PEAS

This wonderfully creamy rice dish is served as a first course in Italy. Give it a try sometime. Risotto is really fun this way and a nice change from soup or salad. But it is also great as a side dish with

< Risotto with Tomatoes and Peas

grilled chicken or fish. We use the Italian arborio rice for this recipe because the grains are short and fat. This allows them to absorb the broth slowly and gives them the desired creamy texture. Look in the specialty rice section in your supermarket as luckily arborio is now fairly available nationwide. If you can't find arborio, use the shortest grain of white rice available.

2 tablespoons olive oil
3 scallions with 1-inch green part, finely chopped
1 cup arborio rice or other short-grain white rice
⅓ cup dry white wine
3 to 3½ cups hot Chicken Stock (page 32) or low-sodium canned chicken broth, heated
2 Roma tomatoes, peeled, seeded, and diced (page 46)
½ cup frozen petite green peas
Salt and freshly ground black pepper, to taste
¼ cup whipping cream
2 tablespoons chopped fresh parsley (preferably Italian flat-leaf)
⅓ cup grated Parmesan cheese

In a 3-quart saucepan, heat olive oil over medium heat. Add chopped scallions and stir with a wooden spoon until soft and translucent, about 3 minutes. Add rice and stir until the grains are well coated with oil, about 1 minute. Add wine and allow it to come to a boil.

Now begin to add the hot chicken stock. Add about ¼ to ⅓ cup stock at a time. Stir it and allow the rice to almost completely absorb the stock before adding more. Adjust the heat under the saucepan so that mixture is kept at a slow bubble. You do not need to stir constantly, but you do want to stick around the kitchen and keep an eye on the pot.

Continue to add more stock and stir frequently until the grains of rice plump and get close to being tender, 20 to 25 minutes. There is no way to test for doneness other than biting on a grain of rice. You want the rice to be tender but not be mushy (*al dente*, with a little bite).

When the rice is nearly at this point, add diced tomatoes, peas, salt and pepper, and cream. Stir well for 1 to 2 minutes, allowing some of the cream to be absorbed. Just before serving, stir in chopped parsley and half the grated cheese. Spoon the risotto into warm bowls, top with the remaining cheese, and serve immediately.
Serves 4.

Cook's Notes

- **Risotto can also make a great main dish with the addition of a little seafood. Cooked small shrimp added just before serving is wonderful. Serve with a green salad and a crusty loaf of French bread.**
- **Substitute fresh asparagus for the peas. Trim the tough ends of the stalks, peel if desired (so they will cook more evenly), and cut into 1/2-inch segments. Add to the pot when beginning to add the hot stock.**

POLENTA

Warm and comforting foods abound in every culture. We certainly would recognize mashed potatoes as one from our culture. But how *about that wonderful Italian import, polenta? Healthy and easy. The New World sent corn to the Italians and they sent us back a fine bowl of steaming polenta. Think of this as an excellent accompaniment when you are serving any braised or roasted meat or fowl.*

1 1/2 cups water
1 1/2 cups milk
1 cup regular-grind yellow cornmeal
1/2 teaspoon salt
Freshly ground black pepper, to taste
About 1/4 cup extra-virgin olive oil
2 tablespoons freshly grated Parmesan cheese (preferably imported)

Bring water and milk to a boil in a 3-quart saucepan. Reduce heat so that the mixture bubbles slowly, but steadily. Stirring constantly with a wooden spoon, drizzle in cornmeal about 1/4 cup at a time, until polenta is the texture of firm mashed potatoes, 20 to 25 minutes. Add salt and pepper. Taste and adjust seasoning.

Portion a generous spoonful onto warm plates. Make a well in the polenta with the back of a spoon. Drizzle a bit of olive oil in the well and sprinkle with grated Parmesan. Serve immediately.
Serves 4.

Cook's Notes

- **Try to plan your meal so you can cook the polenta last. It tends to get pretty thick if made to wait.**

- This may seem like a large saucepan for the amount of polenta, but it can tend to sputter and spatter while you're stirring.

- Instead of serving with olive oil in a well, add $\frac{1}{2}$ cup of grated fontina cheese just before serving and omit the Parmesan.

- Milk as half the liquid adds a nice richness and depth of flavor, but if fat is a strong concern, use all water, or half water and half chicken stock.

- It may be possible to find specially ground polenta corn-meal in your market. Follow directions on your specific package. This meal sometimes requires more water and longer cooking than called for here.

VEGETABLES AND POTATOES

A vegetable primer from A to Z—plus everyone's favorite potato dishes

Understanding and Cooking Fresh Vegetables

Right from the start we will tell you that our preference is to use fresh vegetables whenever possible, but especially when they are the centerpiece of a dish. For us, the deciding factor is quality and taste. Fresh vegetables, when properly prepared, simply taste better, have a far better texture, and look prettier on a plate than their canned or frozen cousins. There are exceptions. For instance, our recipe for glazed baby onions calls for frozen onions. Similarly, a soup might call for a frozen vegetable, or creamed-style corn might be used in a recipe for cornbread. In these cases, the quality of the frozen or canned product is good and therefore recommended. But serving canned asparagus, peas, or green beans, to our way of thinking, is an abomination.

Learn to buy fresh vegetables when they are in season—asparagus in the spring; sugar snap peas, green beans, and corn on the cob in the summer; peppers, eggplant, and squashes in the fall. Of course, with our global markets, we see many more vegetables and fruits year round, but top quality and the best prices are found when the produce is grown closer to home. Learning to cook what is in season brings a harmony and flow to our lives. Most people enjoy a hearty stew during the cold months, whereas a salad of sliced ripe tomatoes, fresh basil, and fresh mozzarella cheese is quintessentially summer. For us, looking forward to the seasons for the bounty they bring is the true joy of food and cooking.

Deciding which method to use for cooking fresh vegetables will depend in part on what else you are preparing for your meal. For instance, if you are grilling your entrée, then it would be easiest to grill a suitable fresh vegetable and have all the cooking happening in the same place. However, if you are braising something in the oven, then cooking a vegetable in water on top of the stove would not complicate the cooking process. Microwaving, in some instances, can be the simplest method, especially if dinner is for just one or two. Following our recommendations for which vegetables work best with a particular cooking technique should ensure success with practice. Before cooking, each vegetable should be prepared (cleaned, cut, etc.) according to the techniques described under specific vegetables throughout this chapter.

Cooking Vegetables in Water

Best for asparagus, broccoli, carrots, cauliflower, corn on the cob, green beans, peas.

Use a pan that is large enough to accommodate the vegetables when they are lying flat. (This especially holds true for asparagus and corn on the cob.) Use a straight-sided frying pan, a 3½ to 4-quart saucepan, or a larger pot, depending on the quantity to be cooked. Use what works best for you. Fill the pan with water about ⅔ full. Bring the water to a boil, add 1 to 2 teaspoons salt (except for corn—salt toughens its tender fibers), then add the prepared vegetable.

< Asparagus with Pine Nuts and Olive Oil

Maintain the heat so that the water continues to simmer. Cook the vegetable until crisp-tender. Typically vegetables cooked in water take anywhere from 3 to 5 minutes to cook. This, however, will take practice and testing. Remove a piece of vegetable and taste; you be the judge. The timing will depend on how the vegetables were cut, the quantity you are cooking, how quickly the water returns to a boil, and so forth. If you don't keep testing the vegetable, you won't know when it is done to your liking. We insist (a pretty strong word to use!) on vegetables being crisp-tender and having a glorious, bright color. This is achieved only when cooked properly. Use tongs or a slotted spoon to remove the vegetable from the water. Drain on paper towels and serve immediately. If using for a salad or as crudités with a dip, plunge the vegetable into a bowl of ice water for 30 seconds, then remove to paper towels to drain.

Steaming Vegetables

Best for asparagus, broccoli, carrots, cauliflower, eggplant, green beans, peas.

Steamer pots and special "stand-up" steaming racks are made for just a particular vegetable. We have never bothered to own this specialized equipment because it seems unnecessary. A simple, collapsible steamer rack that can fit many different-sized pots is all you need for steaming. Select a pot or pan that can hold at least 2 inches of water and, when the steamer rack is in place, the water is below the level of the rack. In addition, the pot or pan must have a tight-fitting lid.

Pour 2 inches of water into pot, cover, and bring water to a boil over high heat. Distribute the prepared vegetables evenly on the rack. Lower rack into pan, replace the lid, and steam. Allow 5 to 7 minutes once the water has returned to a boil and created steam (taste for doneness after about 4 minutes). When vegetables are crisp-tender and still retain a beautiful, bright color, remove pan from heat. Using tongs or a spoon, remove vegetables from rack, place on paper towels to drain, then serve immediately. If using for salad or crudités, plunge into ice water for 30 seconds, then drain.

Microwaving Vegetables

Best for acorn squash, asparagus, broccoli, carrots, cauliflower, corn on the cob, peas.

The only trick with a microwave is that timing varies with quantity. For smaller quantities, it is easy to cook vegetables on a dinner plate. For larger quantities, an oblong glass pan works well. (See page 92 for cooking corn in the microwave and page 88 for acorn squash.) For quantities to serve 1 to 3, place prepared vegetable on a plate, add about 2 tablespoons water, and cover with another plate, a microwavable lid, or plastic wrap. Cook on high power for $2\frac{1}{2}$ to 3 minutes. Test for doneness by tasting a piece of the vegetable. Cook further, depending on your taste. Carefully remove the lid or plastic wrap, drain the water, and serve immediately. Or, if you are serving vegetables cold, dip in ice water for 30 seconds and then pat dry. For larger quantities (say, to serve 4 to 6) allow 3 to 4 minutes of cooking time, then check for doneness. Practice is the best way to fine-tune cooking times for your particular microwave.

Grilling Vegetables

Best for asparagus, corn on the cob, eggplant, mushrooms, onions, bell peppers, zucchini.

Have your grill hot and cut the vegetable to maximize surface exposure to the grill. (See page 92 for specific instructions on cooking corn.) Using a pastry brush, brush the prepared vegetables with a little olive oil, just enough to moisten them, then place the vegetables perpendicular to the slats of the grill rack. Using a spatula or tongs, turn the vegetables as they begin to char lightly. Again test for doneness. Vegetables cooked on the grill generally take about 3 minutes per side. They should still be very crisp when done, but not raw tasting.

Sautéing Vegetables

Best for mushrooms, onions, bell peppers, zucchini. For best results, asparagus, broccoli, carrots, and cauliflower need to be lightly parboiled before sautéing.

Using a 10- to 12-inch frying pan, heat olive oil or butter over medium-high heat. Add prepared vegetables to pan and sauté, stirring frequently, until vegetables are crisp-tender and lightly browned at the edges, about 5 minutes. Parboiled vegetables may need slightly less cooking time. Serve immediately.

Roasting or Braising Vegetables

Best for acorn squash, carrots, eggplant, onions, bell peppers.

Vegetables can be left whole, cut in half, or chunked. Preheat oven to 375°F. To roast, brush vegetables with olive oil or melted butter so that they are lightly coated; season with salt and pepper, if desired. Place in an ovenproof pan or dish and bake for about 45 minutes. Pierce a few vegetables with the tip of a knife to test for doneness. The method for braising vegetables is similar to roasting except, instead of coating the vegetables with oil, a liquid is added to the pan. Typically stock or a tomato sauce is used. Cover the bottom of an ovenproof pan with about 1 inch of liquid, add cut-up vegetables, cover and bake as you would for roasted vegetables. After 30 minutes, baste the vegetables with the liquid. Cover and continue baking until tender.

ACORN SQUASH

Named because of its shape, acorn squash is a delicious winter squash available from early fall until spring. It is considered a "winter" variety, along with pumpkin, butternut, hubbard, turban, and spaghetti squash. Acorn squash is primarily dark green in color on the outside (sometimes with yellow and orange streaks in the skin), smooth to the touch, and weighty. On the inside, the squash is orange. All winter squashes keep well for months stored in a cool dry area.

Basic preparation. Since acorn squash is best baked, braised, or microwaved, its preparation will depend on how it is to be cut for a particular recipe. Acorn squash is cooked with the shell intact. The stem, if still attached, is usually removed and a small slice is taken off the bottom in order for the squash to sit flat in the baking dish. Whether cut in half around the middle, in horizontal slices, or in wedges lengthwise, remove the seeds and stringy pulp surrounding the seeds. At this point the squash is ready to cook.

Acorn Squash Baked with Bourbon

1 acorn squash (about 2 pounds)
$\frac{1}{2}$ teaspoon salt
$\frac{1}{4}$ teaspoon freshly ground black pepper
3 tablespoons unsalted butter
1 tablespoon brown sugar
1 tablespoon bourbon

Preheat oven to 350°F. Slice off and discard top and pointed bottom. Cut squash into horizontal rounds about $\frac{1}{2}$ inch thick and remove seeds and stringy pulp. Lay slices, slightly overlapping, in a baking dish just large enough to hold them. Sprinkle with salt and pepper. In a small saucepan, melt butter and add brown sugar and bourbon, stirring to dissolve sugar. Pour over slices, coating them well. Add 1 tablespoon water to bottom of pan and cover pan with aluminum foil. Twice during the baking time, baste squash with the pan juices. Bake until the tip of a knife is easily inserted into squash, about 45 minutes. Serve immediately, spooning some of the juice over each slice.
Serves 2 or 3.

Cook's Notes

- The squash also can be sliced vertically into wedges for this recipe. Cook cut side up.
- An alternative cooking method is to microwave the squash. Place squash in a microwave-safe dish, proceed with the preparation, cover the pan with plastic wrap, then cook on high power for 7 minutes. Test for doneness and microwave longer if necessary.
- Use pure maple syrup in place of the brown sugar and bourbon and add a touch of lemon juice.
- If watching calories, just use salt, pepper, and some freshly grated nutmeg for seasoning. Acorn squash is naturally sweet.

ASPARAGUS

Buy asparagus when it looks fresh. It will have a lovely green color with no brown spots and the tips will be closed and firm, not mushy. Some people prefer pencil-thin asparagus, others prefer it thick. Try both and decide for yourself. Typically, we serve 5 to 6 spears of asparagus per person. For a salad, we might use as many as 8 per person.

Basic preparation. Rinse asparagus and pat dry. With your hand grasp each spear about $\frac{2}{3}$ of the way down towards the bottom end. Snap or break off end (typically $1\frac{1}{2}$ to 2 inches) and discard. Trim the ends with a knife so they are not ragged. Now comes the true controversy—to peel or not to peel the asparagus. (This is not an issue with pencil-thin asparagus, unless you are a glutton for punishment.) Using a vegetable peeler start at the base of the tip and peel down towards the bottom of the spear. A gentle touch takes off only the fibrous outer layer. Now the asparagus is ready for cooking.

Asparagus with Pine Nuts and Olive Oil

1 pound fresh asparagus
1/4 cup pine nuts
1/2 teaspoon salt, plus 2 teaspoons for the cooking water
1/2 teaspoon freshly ground black pepper
1/4 teaspoon granulated sugar
1/4 cup extra-virgin olive oil

Prepare asparagus as described above and set aside. Heat a small, heavy-bottomed frying pan over medium-high heat; when hot add pine nuts and stir constantly until lightly browned. Remove to a plate to cool. In a measuring cup, combine the 1/2 teaspoon salt, pepper, sugar, and olive oil, stirring to dissolve sugar; set aside.

Select a pan large enough to accommodate the asparagus when it's lying flat. A straight-sided frying pan, or a 3 1/2- to 4-quart saucepan will work well. Fill pan with water about 2/3 full. About 10 minutes before serving, bring the water to a boil, add 2 teaspoons salt, then add prepared asparagus. Lower heat to a slow boil and cook asparagus 3 minutes. Then remove a spear and cut a piece to taste for doneness. You be the judge; the timing will depend on the thickness of the asparagus, the quantity cooked, and so forth. Our preference is for asparagus cooked crisp-tender and maintaining a beautiful green color. Use tongs to remove asparagus from water, drain on paper towels, and place spears on a warmed serving plate. Stir olive oil mixture, pour over asparagus, and sprinkle pine nuts on top. Serve immediately.
Serves 4 or 5.

Cook's Notes

- The flavoring ingredients listed above can still be used if you choose to cook the asparagus in the microwave, on the grill, or in a steamer. See Understanding and Cooking Fresh Vegetables (page 85), for these alternative cooking methods.
- Some people like a squeeze of lemon juice on their asparagus. Be forewarned, however, that lemon juice turns asparagus a yellowish-brown color; so serve lemon wedges on the side.
- Substitute for the pine nuts other chopped and toasted nuts (such as almonds, walnuts, or hazelnuts) or freshly grated Parmesan cheese.
- Use melted butter in place of the olive oil.

BROCCOLI

Like cauliflower, broccoli is a member of the cabbage family. Despite some bad press from people in high places, broccoli is quite delicious and everyone agrees that it is good for you. Look for tightly closed buds of a deep green or purplish green color. Avoid tops that are somewhat yellow-green and buds that are slightly open rather than tightly closed.

pieces first for 4 to 5 minutes, then add florets and steam until broccoli is as tender as you like it, about 5 minutes. Turn off heat, drain, and keep warm until serving.

Heat olive oil in an 8-inch frying pan over medium heat. Add garlic and cook until the garlic turns golden, 2 to 3 minutes. Do not let the garlic burn. Place broccoli in a serving dish and pour garlic-oil mixture over it. Season to taste and serve.
Serves 4 to 6.

CAULIFLOWER

Look for very white, firm heads. Avoid cauliflower that has brown spots, looks yellow, or has wide spaces between the stems — it is past its prime. Cauliflower has become more popular raw than cooked in recent years, so you really want to pick fresh heads.

Basic preparation. Cut off the hard part of the stem and break the cauliflower into clumps. Trim off excess stem to make florets. Wash and drain; a colander is a great way to do this. Raw florets will keep in a zipper-top plastic bag up to 2 days in the refrigerator. If not eating cauliflower raw in salad or with a dip, steaming is the best way to cook it.

Cauliflower with Brown Butter and Parmesan

   1 medium head cauliflower (about 1 1/2 pounds)
   1/2 stick (4 tablespoons) unsalted butter

Basic preparation. Wash in a colander and let drain. Trim the stem and discard the hard end. The florets will cook faster than the stems, but you can peel the stem down to a pale green tender part with a swivel-action vegetable peeler. The florets are great steamed and the stems can be sliced and used in stir-fry dishes and soups. The peeled stems can also be steamed, adding them first to the pot for 4 to 5 minutes, then adding the tops.

Broccoli with Garlic and Olive Oil

   1 pound broccoli spears
   2 tablespoons olive oil
   2 small cloves garlic, peeled and very finely minced
   Salt and freshly ground black pepper, to taste

Wash and trim broccoli as directed above. Cut stem pieces lengthwise into "sticks" and separate head into florets. Steam, according to instructions on page 86. Cook stem

2 tablespoons freshly grated Parmesan cheese

Salt and freshly ground black pepper, to taste

Break head into clumps and wash as directed above. Steam over boiling water, as directed on page 86, until cauliflower is as tender or as firm as you like it, about 10 to 15 minutes. Drain, place in a serving bowl, and cover with aluminum foil to keep hot.

In a 1-quart saucepan, melt and brown butter over medium heat until it foams and turns dark and brown. Immediately pour it over cauliflower and sprinkle with Parmesan cheese. Season to taste.

Serves 4.

Cook's Notes

◆ **Brown or "burnt" butter gives an unusual but delicious flavor to all sorts of dishes. You must use butter; margarine will not work in this instance. If you find you like the flavor, and we believe you will, brown butter can be used over other vegetables: green beans, asparagus, broccoli, and the like. It is also delightful served over cooked pasta with freshly grated Parmesan cheese and no other sauce. If brown butter cools off before serving, you can reheat it in the microwave for 1 or 2 minutes, but it should be prepared at the very last minute.**

CORN ON THE COB

The best corn we have ever eaten was cut from the stalk, shucked, and cooked, all within ten minutes. Obviously, this scenario isn't always possible, but freshness is the key when purchasing corn. The closer you can get to the source, the better. We always look for farm stands in the summer; however, if stuck in the city, befriend a green-grocer and buy when fresh. Sweet corn comes in three colors—white, yellow, and a mix of the two. (We have no preference; if fresh, all can be good.) We prefer to buy corn unshucked. Look for grassy green husks that feel silken and slightly damp. Peel back a bit of the husk to be sure the rows of corn have even, plump kernels. New varieties of corn called "super-sweet" have been developed with higher levels of naturally occurring sugars. These varieties are reliably good.

Basic preparation. Keep corn unshucked and refrigerated until ready to use. Peel back the green husks and silk surrounding the corn and discard (but not down your drain!). Trim the base of the cob if necessary. The corn is now ready to cook.

Corn on the Cob with Chili Butter or Herbed Butter

Chili Butter

1 stick (¼ pound) unsalted butter, at room temperature

½ teaspoon chili powder

Pinch cayenne pepper

¼ teaspoon granulated sugar

¼ teaspoon salt

2 tablespoons minced fresh cilantro

Herbed Butter

1 stick (¼ pound) unsalted butter, at room temperature

2 tablespoons minced fresh parsley

2 teaspoons minced fresh tarragon or 1 teaspoon dried tarragon

2 teaspoons freshly grated Parmesan cheese

¼ teaspoon salt

⅛ teaspoon freshly ground black pepper

1 ear of corn per person

Prepare either the Chili Butter or Herbed Butter, or both, by mixing thoroughly the butter and seasonings in a small bowl with a rubber spatula. Or use a food processor if you have one. Pack each flavored butter into a small crock, individual soufflé dish, or small bowl. Cover with plastic wrap and set aside until ready to use. Or make ahead and refrigerate up to 3 days. Bring to room temperature before serving.

Prepare corn as directed above. Use a pot large enough to accommodate the amount of corn you are planning to cook. Fill pot ⅔ full with water. Cover, place over high heat, and bring water to a full rolling boil. Five minutes before serving, add corn to the boiling water, 1 ear at a time (to prevent the boiling water from splashing), and cook, uncovered, for 5 minutes total. Remove corn using tongs, drain on paper towels, and serve immediately. Accompany corn with the flavored butters.

Each flavored butter makes about ½ cup and serves 8.

Cook's Notes

- Handy to have, but not essential, are corn holders. These act as small handles on each end of an ear of corn. Little prongs stick into each end to secure the holders. The corn eater holds onto the handles rather than the hot edges of the corn!

- Leftover Chili Butter or Herbed Butter can be refrigerated or frozen. Use these flavored butters on baked potatoes, in mashed potatoes, and in "oven-fried" potatoes. The Herbed Butter along with additional Parmesan is good on stuffed pasta such as ravioli or tortellini.

- Alternative cooking methods for corn on the cob include grilling, roasting in the oven, and microwaving. For the grill or the oven (preheated to 475°F), pull down the husk, remove silk, then replace the husk. Run water into the corn, drain excess, then twist the husk closed at the top. Grill or roast about 20 minutes. For the microwave, prepare corn as just described; on high power, microwave 1 ear for 2 minutes, 2 ears for 5 minutes, and 4 ears for 9 minutes.

EGGPLANT

Typically, there are two types of eggplant found in the market. The most common eggplant is the large, thick-skinned, dark-purple globular variety. Chinese or Japanese eggplant is small (about 5 to 6 inches long and 1 inch in diameter), dark to light purple in color, and has a slightly thinner skin. Whichever you buy, pick eggplant that is firm, without any bruised spots on it, and that does not have too much green color around the stem end (which indicates it is not ripe).

Basic Preparation. Depending on the requirements for a particular recipe, eggplants may need to be peeled, salted, and/or soaked in ice water. For peeling, a swivel-action vegetable peeler works well, removing the peel in long strokes from top to bottom. Eggplants retain a lot of moisture; salting slices or cubes of eggplant, then placing them in a colander for 30 minutes, allows the moisture to be released. Drain, rinse, and pat dry the cubes or slices with paper towels before proceeding. This preparation is usually called for when eggplant is to be sautéed or baked. If a recipe calls for eggplant to be soaked, it is because the large, globular eggplants can be bitter.

Eggplant Simply Grilled

1 large eggplant or several small eggplants (about 1 pound total)

⅓ cup olive oil

½ teaspoon salt

Freshly ground black pepper, to taste

Prepare grill and have coals hot. Slice off the stem of eggplant and discard. Slice large eggplant crosswise into ½-inch-thick rounds. (If using the small variety, slice in half lengthwise.) Lay slices in a single layer on a pan or baking sheet. Brush each slice on both sides with olive oil. Sprinkle salt and pepper on top side of each slice. Place on grill in a single layer. Cook on one side, until nicely browned, about 4 minutes. Turn and cook on other side about 3 minutes.

Serve immediately.

Serves 4.

Cook's Notes

◆ Use this same technique to grill vegetables such as zucchini, bell peppers, sliced onions, and asparagus.

◆ Grilling vegetables works well when you are already using the grill to cook poultry, beef, or seafood.

◆ To use grilled eggplant to make an interesting first course, slice lengthwise instead. Place some softened goat cheese and a fresh basil leaf on one end of the grilled eggplant, roll up to enclose filling, place 2 rolls on a plate and top with some Fresh Tomato Sauce (page 67), or Cooked Tomato Sauce (page 66). Serve at room temperature, along with some crusty French or Italian bread.

GREEN BEANS

Green beans are a seasonal vegetable in most of the United States. They can be found year round, but the quality is not worth the price. Frozen green beans are a better choice when good quality fresh ones are not available. Look for a medium-dark green color without big beans showing through the skin. The thinner they are, the more tender they will be. When buying frozen beans, buy cut green beans, not French cut, which become mushy and overcooked very quickly.

Basic preparation. When using fresh beans, cut off the stem ends, wash, and drain in a colander. Beans can be cooked whole or cut in half or thirds, depending on the length. Sometimes when you cut the stem end a "string" will come with it from along the seam. Pull it out, but not all green beans have strings. (Guess where the name "string beans" came from?) Green beans are delicious steamed or boiled, served with butter and seasoning. If you are more adventuresome, we offer a green bean stew made with tomatoes.

Spicy Green Beans in Tomato Sauce

2 tablespoons olive oil

1 clove garlic, peeled and minced

1 medium-size yellow onion (about 5 ounces), peeled and diced

3/4 pound fresh green beans, stemmed and cut in half crosswise, or 1 package (20 ounces) frozen cut green beans

1 can (14 1/2 ounces) peeled, diced tomatoes with liquid

1/2-inch piece cinnamon stick

1 bay leaf

1 tablespoon minced fresh mint

1/4 teaspoon granulated sugar

Salt and freshly ground black pepper, to taste

Heat olive oil in a heavy 4-quart saucepan over medium heat. Add garlic and onion, and sauté until soft and translucent, 3 to 4 minutes. Add beans, tomatoes, cinnamon stick, bay leaf, mint, and sugar. Add salt and pepper to taste.

Bring mixture to a boil, reduce heat to low, and cook, covered, until beans are tender but still crisp, about 1/2 hour. Remove bay leaf before serving.

Serves 4 to 6.

Cook's Notes

- ◆ If you have vine-ripened fresh tomatoes, use 1 pound, peeled, seeded, and diced. Otherwise, canned are much better than off-season tomatoes, which have no taste and are not juicy.
- ◆ Add 1/2 pound small red potatoes, unpeeled, with the green beans for a tasty one-dish accompaniment to meat or fish.

MUSHROOMS

If using the common domestic mushrooms—either the white button varieties or the brown cremini mushrooms—look for tightly closed caps and no soft spots. If using wild or more exotic mushrooms such as chanterelle, morel, oyster, or shiitake, look for plump (as opposed to shriveled) tops and fresh-looking edges. Brown spots or mold will develop on wild mushrooms that are too old; avoid those. Store mushrooms loosely wrapped in paper towels, loosely stored in a plastic bag in the refrigerator. Plan to use mushrooms within two days of purchase.

Basic preparation. Wipe mushrooms clean with a damp paper towel. Mushrooms act like sponges absorbing water, so washing mushrooms under running water will result in a diluted, watery taste. Using a sharp paring knife, trim the ends of the stem and any ragged edges of the cap. Dice, slice, or leave mushrooms whole, according to the recipe directions.

Mushrooms Sautéed with Onions and Fresh Herbs   >

Mushrooms Sautéed with Onions and Fresh Herbs

1 tablespoon chopped fresh sage

1 tablespoon fresh thyme leaves

2 tablespoons minced fresh parsley

2 tablespoons olive oil

2 tablespoons unsalted butter

1 pound large, fresh domestic or wild mushrooms, cleaned, trimmed, and sliced

1 medium-size yellow onion (about 8 ounces), peeled and cut into thin wedges

$^{1}/_{2}$ teaspoon salt

$^{1}/_{4}$ teaspoon freshly ground black pepper

2 tablespoons pale dry sherry

In a small bowl, combine sage, thyme, and parsley and set aside. Heat a large frying pan over high heat. Add olive oil and butter. When hot, add mushrooms and onions. Sauté, stirring frequently, until tender and lightly browned, 5 to 7 minutes. Add fresh herbs, then add salt, pepper, and sherry; stir to combine. Serve immediately in a warmed bowl or on warmed plates.

Serves 4 or 5.

Cook's Notes

◆ **This recipe is best if cooked right before serving. However, the ingredients can be prepared in advance. Mushrooms can be prepared up to 2 hours ahead, sprinkled with a little lemon juice, and covered with a damp paper towel.**

◆ **Sautéed mushrooms are a wonderful accompaniment to roasted poultry and meats.**

◆ **This recipe is at its best when fresh herbs are used. If fresh sage and thyme are unavailable, use 1 teaspoon each dried sage and thyme mixed with the sherry to bring out more of the herbs' flavors.**

◆ **Substitute red onion or sweet onions (Vidalia or Walla Walla) when in season.**

◆ **Toss this mixture with cooked fettuccine ($^{3}/_{4}$ to 1 pound), adding a little of the pasta cooking water and $^{1}/_{2}$ cup of cream (optional), for a meatless entrée or side dish.**

◆ **Use any leftovers as the filling in an omelet.**

GLAZED BABY ONIONS

As you have probably noticed by now, we are strong advocates of using fresh foods as much as possible, especially vegetables and fruits. However, there are some instances when frozen vegetables are very useful. You could buy tiny boiling onions and peel them all—a tedious task, to say the least. But why should you, when frozen whole baby onions are available in your supermarket? These are so delicious you will probably find yourself eating any leftovers as you clean up the kitchen—we do.

1 package (16 ounces) frozen whole baby onions, thawed

2 tablespoons unsalted butter

3 tablespoons brown sugar

1 tablespoon balsamic vinegar

Salt and freshly ground black pepper, to taste

Melt butter in a 10-inch frying pan over medium heat until it begins to foam. Add onions and cook, stirring frequently, until onions are well coated and translucent, about 7 minutes. Reduce heat to low, add brown sugar, and stir, being careful not to crush onions. Cook until sugar caramelizes and onions are tender, about 15 minutes. Add vinegar and cook another 3 to 4 minutes. Season with salt and pepper and serve. *Serves 4 to 6.*

Cook's Notes

♦   **If you are not able to find balsamic vinegar, you may use apple cider vinegar. The flavor is not quite the same, but it can be used as a substitute. Balsamic vinegar comes from Italy and is aged in oak casks. It is very mellow and not sharp-tasting. It is well worth searching out because it can be used in many ways and is great in basic vinaigrette.**

SWEET AND HOT PEPPERS

Vegetable peppers come in two varieties, sweet and hot. Most sweet peppers are also called "bell" peppers by virtue of their shape. Not too long ago most markets carried only green and red bell peppers (red ones being just a riper version of the green). But now greengrocers are stocking yellow, orange, and even purple bell peppers as well. Hot peppers are known as chili peppers and grow in various shapes and sizes. They have widely differing degrees of heat. Typically, the smaller they are, the hotter they tend to be. Jalapeños, serranos, and Anaheims are just some of the varieties of fresh chili peppers available;

ask the produce buyer for help if the peppers are not labeled clearly. When shopping for peppers, buy those that are bright in color and firm. Soft spots or shriveled skin is an indication of a pepper past its peak. Keep peppers under refrigeration until ready to use. Red bell peppers have a shorter shelf life, so don't buy too far ahead of using them.

Basic preparation. Regardless of the recipe, all peppers (both sweet and hot) need to be rinsed, cored, seeded, and deveined by removing the white membrane. (Some people, when using hot chili peppers, like to use the seeds for additional heat in a dish—that is up to you.) Use a paring knife to cut around the core, lift out, and discard. If you are using the peppers whole, say for stuffed peppers, tap or rinse out the seeds and use your fingers to peel away the white membrane. Otherwise, cut the peppers in half to remove more easily the seeds and membrane. Cut the peppers according to recipe directions.

Sweet Bell Pepper Sauté

$1\frac{1}{4}$ pounds red, orange, or yellow bell peppers (or a combination)

1 green bell pepper (about 6 ounces)

3 tablespoons olive oil

1 large yellow onion (about 12 ounces) peeled and cut into thin wedges

$\frac{3}{4}$ teaspoon salt

$\frac{1}{2}$ teaspoon granulated sugar

$\frac{1}{2}$ teaspoon freshly ground black pepper

Core, seed, and devein bell peppers; then cut into thin wedges. Heat a 10-inch frying pan over high heat. Add olive oil and swirl to coat the bottom of pan. Add onion and peppers and sauté, stirring constantly, about 5 minutes. Add salt, sugar, and pepper. Continue sautéing until onions and peppers are tender and lightly browned at the edges, about 2 minutes. Serve immediately.

Serves 6.

Cook's Notes

- **If you would like some fire, add a finely minced jalapeño chili along with the bell peppers. Adding a finely chopped Anaheim chili would add a more moderate amount of heat. Experiment, add a little, and taste. You can always add more.**
- **This recipe is best when freshly sautéed, but it does reheat well for leftovers.**
- **Use any leftovers along with some shredded Monterey jack cheese as a filling for omelets.**

ZUCCHINI AND OTHER SUMMER SQUASH

Zucchini is a slender, dark-green summer squash. Other summer squashes include yellow crookneck or straight neck and the scallop-edged pattypan. Despite its seasonal classification, zucchini is available in the market year round. Summer squashes, though different in shape, are all thin skinned, and can be used interchangeably or in combination in a recipe. Look for zucchini and crookneck that are small (about 4 to 5 inches long), feel firm, and are heavy for their size. The pattypan should be no wider than 3 inches in diameter. Summer squashes do not store well, so refrigerate and plan to use within 1 to 2 days of purchase.

Basic preparation. Summer squash requires very little preparation. Wipe clean and trim at both ends. Do not peel or remove the seeds unless the recipe specifies to do so. Cut as directed in recipe: Zucchini and crookneck are usually sliced crosswise for boiling or sautéing or sliced lengthwise for broiling or grilling. Pattypans are usually cut into wedges.

Zucchini Sautéed with Basil

3 medium zucchini (about 1 pound)
3 tablespoons olive oil
$1/2$ teaspoon salt
$1/4$ teaspoon freshly ground black pepper
2 tablespoons chopped fresh basil

Slice zucchini into $1/4$-inch-thick rounds. In a 12-inch frying pan, heat olive oil over medium-high heat for about 30 seconds. Add zucchini to pan and sauté, stirring continuously, until zucchini are crisp-tender and lightly browned at the edges, about 5 minutes. Add salt, pepper, and basil to pan; continue cooking 1 to 2 minutes more. Serve immediately.
Serves 4.

Cook's Notes

- **Substitute any variety of summer squash in this recipe, or use a combination for color contrast.**
- **Sautéed zucchini is at its best right from the pan; we don't recommend holding it or trying to rewarm it while other dinner preparations are being completed. Prepare it last.**
- **Substitute other fresh herbs or use a combination.**

Parsley, oregano, marjoram, even a little mint, go nicely with summer squash.

- **Sprinkle some freshly grated Parmesan cheese over the top.**
- **Add some thin wedges of onion while you are sautéing the zucchini. In addition, thin wedges of peeled and seeded Roma tomatoes can be added during the last 2 minutes of cooking.**

TYPES OF POTATOES AND BASIC COOKING DIRECTIONS

Potatoes are tubers, which means the vegetable itself grows underground and only the green leaves are visible above the surface. Basically, there are three types of potatoes: the red, beige, or yellow waxy kind, suitable for boiling; the brown russets or Idaho potatoes, for baking and mashing; and sweet potatoes or yams. Let's discuss them, one group at a time.

Waxy Potatoes

These have a very thin smooth skin and remain firm when they are cooked—as long as you do not overcook them. Within this category there are three kinds: those with red skins called "Red Rose"; those with whitish-beige skins known as "White Rose" or "Shafters"; and yellow ones usually called "Finnish" or "Yukon Gold." (These potatoes are pale yellow and are very interesting in potato salad when mixed with white ones.) The taste and texture is similar in all three. When harvested young and small, waxy potatoes are often marketed as "new potatoes." The waxy varieties are great for boiling, for use in potato and other cold salads, and for roasting whole in the oven.

Boiled waxy potatoes. To peel or not to peel is the question. It is simply a matter of your own preference. Small whole red potatoes are very attractive when the skin is left on or a thin strip is peeled around the middle only. Scrub potatoes with a brush and peel them if you like. Place in a saucepan with water to cover, bring to a boil, cover, reduce heat, and simmer until tender when pierced with a fork, 20 to 30 minutes; do not overcook or they will fall apart. When using boiled potatoes for a salad, drain and rinse in cold water immediately to stop the cooking process. An easy and delicious way to serve boiled potatoes is to drain them when finished cooking, return them to the pot, add 1 or 2 tablespoons butter, cover the pot and allow the butter to melt on them with the heat off for 1 or 2 minutes. Place in a serving bowl and garnish with minced fresh parsley.

Russet or Idaho Potatoes

These have a thick brown grainy skin and are perfect for baking, for mashing, and for French fries, because they are dry and fluffy when cooked and, for fries, do not absorb as much oil as the waxy varieties.

Baked russet potatoes. Preheat oven to 400°F. Scrub skins with a stiff brush, pierce completely through once with a sharp knife (to keep them from bursting in the oven), and rub skin with vegetable oil. (If you have never had a potato explode all over your oven, you don't want to!) Bake directly on the oven rack in the middle of the oven for 45 to 60 minutes. They should be soft to the touch when squeezed gently. Potatoes can also be baked in a microwave. They cook much faster, but they become more like steamed potatoes than baked. Prepare them the same way as for oven baking, including piercing them all the way through. Cook on high power. Allow 4 to 6 minutes for 1 potato and 6 to 8 minutes for 2.

Oven-fried potatoes. Since French fries are the favorite American way to eat potatoes, we have developed an oven-fried method to eliminate frying and grease. Preheat oven to 425°F and place the oven rack in the middle of the oven. Peel russet potatoes and cut into quarters lengthwise; then cut each quarter lengthwise into wedge-shaped pieces. Coat each potato with 1 tablespoon olive oil mixed with 1 tablespoon water. Place them in a single layer in a baking pan coated with nonstick cooking spray. Bake for 20 minutes, then turn on the broiler, leaving the pan on the middle rack of the oven. Broil until they turn brown and crispy, usually 5 to 10 minutes. Watch them so they don't burn. Season to taste: salt and pepper are standard, but a touch of cayenne or chili powder, a seasoned salt, or crush dried herbs are great. If you have a gas oven with the broiler underneath your oven rather than on top, do not broil them as they may burn. Continue cooking in the middle of the oven until they turn brown and crispy. It may take 5 minutes longer by this method.

Sweet Potatoes and Yams

Sweet potatoes—yams—what's the difference? Yes, Virginia, there is indeed a difference. Sweet potatoes have a pale gold skin and flesh and are delicious baked, boiled, or mashed; they are more like russets in texture when cooked. The variety of sweet potato marketed as a yam is larger, with reddish-brown skin; the flesh is dark orange, denser, and somewhat waxy. Either variety can be baked, much the same as russets, but most people don't eat the skin of yams.

Baked sweet potatoes and yams. Preheat oven to 400°F. Scrub potatoes well, pierce with a knife, and rub the skin with vegetable oil. Bake until soft to the touch when squeezed gently. Since sweet potatoes are usually small, they will cook in 35 to 40 minutes; yams will take longer, 50 to 70 minutes, depending on the size.

MASHED POTATOES

We're willing to bet that mashed potatoes are on your list of comfort foods. Maybe your mother served up a creamy bowl of freshly made mashed potatoes to accompany the turkey to your holiday table; or perhaps they usually appeared nestled alongside the liver and onions she was trying to get you to eat! Or, sadly, maybe you've experienced only the rehydrated instant glop served up in lots of restaurants which ought to know better—often coming out of an instant hot cocoa–type machine! Do yourself a favor and make our version. You won't want the instant stuff anymore.

> 2 to 3 large russet potatoes (8 to 10 ounces each)
> ½ to ⅔ cups milk
> ½ stick (4 tablespoons) unsalted butter
> Salt and freshly ground black pepper, to taste

Peel and rinse potatoes. Cut each into 4 or 5 large chunks and place in a 3- to 4-quart saucepan. Cover with cold water, cover pot, and bring the water to a boil. Uncover and reduce heat so water boils gently. Cook until potato chunks feel tender but not mushy when pierced with a fork, 10 to 12 minutes. Do not cook until they are soft and mushy or they will be watery and might even start to disintegrate in the water! Meanwhile heat milk and butter together in a small saucepan until hot but not boiling.

Drain potatoes and place back in the warm pan over low heat for 1 to 2 minutes to evaporate excess water. Remove from heat and mash potatoes in the pan using any masher or even a well-constructed wire whisk; or pass them through any of several potato ricers built for the job. Whisk the milk and butter mixture into potatoes a bit at a time, until they are as soft and moist as you like. If potatoes are too dry, add a little more hot milk. Add salt and pepper to taste.
Serves 4.

Cook's Notes

- **Potatoes may be cooked and mashed 30 to 45 minutes in advance and kept warm in a covered heatproof glass or stainless steel bowl set over barely simmering water in a saucepan. Or they may be reheated just before serving in a glass or plastic bowl in a microwave oven.**
- **Add ½ cup freshly grated Parmesan cheese.**
- **Heat 2 or 3 crushed cloves fresh garlic with the milk and butter. Allow to stand 10 minutes, then strain out when adding milk to potatoes.**

SCALLOPED POTATOES

Our idea of heaven with meat loaf, roasted meat, or fowl—one of us even would eat them for breakfast! Scalloped potatoes involve very little more than greasing a baking dish, slicing some potatoes, and opening a carton of milk. Can you find the mail in your mailbox? If you can, then you can make these. It's even more fun and you can eat them too!

Nonstick cooking spray
4 to 5 large russet potatoes (about 3 pounds total)
3 to 4 cups milk
Few grinds black pepper
Salt to taste (about 1 teaspoon)

Preheat oven to 350°F. Spray a 9x13-inch glass baking dish with nonstick spray.

Peel potatoes and cut into medium slices, about ⅙ inch (a 4 mm food processor slicing disc works very well). Layer slices in slightly overlapping fashion in the prepared baking dish. Pour enough milk over potatoes to barely cover them. Top with freshly ground pepper and sprinkle with salt. Bake uncovered until potatoes are cooked and the milk has been absorbed; time varies depending on the potatoes and your oven, but 1 hour and 15 minutes to 1 hour and 45 minutes will probably be close. The cooked potatoes can be covered with aluminum foil and held for up to ½ hour before serving. Leftovers reheat well.
Serves 8 or more.

- **Substitute whipping cream for part or all of the milk— your arteries will recoil in horror, your brain will love it! Layer some onion slices in with the potatoes. Sprinkle some grated cheese in. Add some herbs or fresh garlic slices. Substitute beef or chicken broth for some of the milk. You get the idea; smile and experiment. Cooking time varies according to ingredients.**

HASHED BROWN POTATOES

Universally popular, hashed browns are a fine accompaniment to all manner of main dishes. Serve them for breakfast with egg dishes or pair them with an elegant grilled tenderloin steak; they do well in casual or dress-up clothes, so to speak! Hashed browns can be several different things in America, among them: grated, uncooked potatoes formed into patties and sautéed; cooked potatoes grated while warm, formed into patties or large pancake shapes and sautéed; raw peeled or unpeeled potatoes coarsely chopped and sautéed; and leftover cooked potatoes, coarsely chopped and sautéed. We've tried them all and most often choose the latter style.

2 to 3 russet potatoes (1 to 1½ pounds), baked or boiled until tender
3 tablespoons unsalted butter or vegetable oil
Salt and freshly ground black pepper, to taste

Coarsely chop cooked potatoes (we usually leave on the skins). Heat butter or oil over medium-high heat in a 10- or 12-inch frying pan. Add potatoes and cook until they have browned a little on the bottom. Turn potatoes using a stiff spatula, scraping any brown residue from the bottom. Cook potatoes until they brown further, turning and mixing occasionally. When potatoes are browned to your liking, add salt and pepper.

Serves 2 to 4.

Cook's Notes

- **A heavyweight nonstick frying pan makes turning potatoes easier; on the other hand, they tend to brown fastest in a cast iron skillet or other heavyweight plain metal frying pan.**
- **Add 1 cup coarsely chopped or diced yellow onions. Toss with potatoes before cooking.**
- **Add ¼ cup chopped fresh herbs of your choice.**
- **Sprinkle 1 cup shredded Cheddar or Swiss cheese over browned potatoes and broil until cheese is bubbly.**
- **Add 1 to 2 cups coarsely chopped leftover cooked meat or poultry, 1 rib sliced or diced celery, and 1 cup coarsely chopped yellow onion. The resulting hash is a main dish on its own; season any way you like. Try served with a poached egg on top and ketchup bottle at the ready!**

SEAFOOD AND POULTRY

Mostly quick, light, and low-fat—baked, poached, steamed, and stir-fried

BUYING FRESH FISH AND SHELLFISH

A good seafood meal starts with fresh, well-cared-for fish or shellfish. Sounds like a simple proposition and it ought to be. Unfortunately, there are still lots of people who are not sure how to buy foods that come with fins or shells attached! Worse, there are still lots of markets selling old, smelly fish to people who think all fish smells. It matters not whether your fish comes from a huge supermarket or a tiny corner fish market; the basics are always the same.

Don't buy fish or shellfish in prewrapped packages if at all possible. Go to a market that displays its catch in an open, refrigerated case. If the market has a really strong fish odor (old, fishy, rather than fresh, smelling like the sea), try somewhere else. Look for moist, almost glistening fish; if the surface doesn't look moist and the edges are dry, the fish is likely to be old (maybe even frozen and thawed) and taste like it. Look for shellfish that does not have lots of open shells with dried-out looking meats inside (slightly open shells not showing dried-out meats are OK). If you have any doubts about the freshness of what you are buying, ask to smell it. A fish market that will not let you smell your purchase in advance doesn't deserve your business. Buy previously frozen fish only if you have no alternative.

Patronize a good fish and shellfish market regularly and get friendly with the counter clerk. He or she will be more likely to steer you to the freshest and best as a result.

GRILLED FISH STEAKS AND FILLETS

Food cooked over an open fire or on an outdoor grill is often more memorable than the same food cooked indoors. The sweet, gentle flavor of really fresh fish marries beautifully with the smoke produced by grilling it (cooking over hot coals or lava rocks). Grilling is our favorite method of cooking fish steaks and fillets and most often we serve them unsauced. Good candidates for the grill include salmon, tuna, marlin, swordfish, sturgeon, halibut, ling cod, and shark, among others. Steaks, by the way, are cut across the bone; fillets are cut parallel to the bone and skin.

$\frac{1}{4}$ to $\frac{1}{2}$ pound fresh fish steaks or fillets ($\frac{3}{4}$ inch to 1 inch thick), per person
About 2 teaspoons olive oil or vegetable oil, for each piece of fish
Salt and freshly ground black pepper, to taste

Build a charcoal fire in your usual way or preheat your gas grill. When the coals are covered in a fine, white ash, spread them in a single layer. Rub a little oil over both sides of the fish. (Fillets may be cooked with skin on or off; we usually cook them with the skin on, as it is easily removed after cooking.)

Place fish on the cooking grid, season with salt and pepper, and clap the ventilated lid on the grill to trap the smoke.

< Roast Chicken

Total cooking time will approximate 10 minutes per inch of thickness. Turn steaks in half this time. You may turn fillets, or, if they are not several inches thick, just cook on the skin side until done. This helps avoid broken-up fillets caused by turning. Check doneness using an instant-read thermometer inserted in the thickest part of the fish. We like ours quite moist and pull it off the grill at 120°F. If you prefer your fish a little drier, with a bit more chew, wait for 140°F.

Cook's Notes

◆ **Each brand of grill is different in shape and construction. Better, more expensive brands have flatter, more closely spaced cooking grids, which helps prevent small or flaky bits of food like fish from falling into the coals. Other brands have broader spaced, round wire cooking grids, which can make it difficult to cook softer fish varieties. If you own one of these, you can purchase a flat, perforated, porcelainized grid to lay over your regular cooking grid. It allows you to cook small items like shrimp or scallops, as well as soft-fleshed fish, with less loss to the fire.**

◆ **Fish can be marinated in all manner of mixtures before cooking. Try 2 tablespoons fresh lemon or lime juice mixed with 2 teaspoons soy sauce and 1/4 cup olive or vegetable oil. Marinate fish on both sides, totaling 20 to 30 minutes. Cook as above, skipping the oiling step and basting once on each side with the marinade.**

◆ **Brush fish with the following mixture before grilling: 1 tablespoon Dijon-style mustard, 3 tablespoons olive oil or vegetable oil, a few grinds pepper, 1 tablespoon chopped fresh tarragon or 1 teaspoon dried tarragon.**

SAUTÉED SCALLOPS

Sweet and succulent, this simple sauté offers an almost instant dinner. Serve with Basmati Rice Pilaf (page 77) and Spicy Green Beans in Tomato Sauce (page 94) and you have a dinner fit for the boss.

3/4 pound scallops
1/4 cup all-purpose flour
1/4 teaspoon cayenne pepper
1/4 teaspoon salt
Freshly ground black pepper
2 tablespoons unsalted butter

Rinse scallops in a colander and drain. Pat dry with paper towels. If they are large sea scallops, cut in half. Place flour, cayenne, salt, and black pepper in a medium bowl. Preheat a 10-inch frying pan (preferably nonstick) over high heat. While the pan is heating, toss scallops in flour mixture.

Test the pan for heat by sprinkling a little water on it. If the water immediately beads and dances, it is hot. Add butter. It will melt very quickly. As soon as melted, toss in scallops by shaking them in your hand to remove excess flour. Stay close to the pan at this point. The sauté will happen very quickly. Allow the scallops to brown on one side for about 30 seconds and then stir about each 30 seconds after that. Total cooking time will be 2 to 3 minutes only. Cook until scallops feel just firm to the touch and are barely opaque in the center. We do not mind seeing just a bit of translucency if the scallop is cut open. Serve immediately on warm plates.

Serves 2.

Cook's Notes

- If doubling the recipe to serve 4, use two 10-inch frying pans or quickly cook 2 batches, one after the other.
- If using tiny bay scallops, cooking time will be barely 2 minutes. Whatever you do, be very careful not to overcook. Scallops are wonderful when tender, but rubbery if cooked too long.

SAUTÉED SOLE FILLETS

Few white-fleshed fish have achieved the popularity of sole over the centuries. Actually, the fish called "soles" are different species in different parts of the world. Regardless of the names, the several varieties marketed as sole on the American coasts and in better inland fish markets are tempting fare indeed. They have an innate sweetness of flavor and a characteristic lack of "fishy" flavor which have made them stars on great restaurants' menus forever. Whether called "Dover," "English," petrale, rex and sand dabs (both usually sold whole), lemon, or some other name, sole fillets (or small whole fish) are easy cooking and wonderful eating.

About $1\frac{1}{4}$ pounds sole fillets (or 1 to 2 small whole soles, per person)

$\frac{1}{4}$ cup all-purpose flour, for dredging

Salt and freshly ground black pepper, to taste

$\frac{3}{4}$ stick (6 tablespoons) unsalted butter

2 tablespoons dry vermouth or other white wine

$\frac{1}{4}$ cup chopped fresh parsley

Dry fillets on paper towels. Place flour, salt, and pepper in a gallon-size plastic or paper bag and shake to combine. Just before you are ready to sauté, add 1 or more of the fillets to the bag to coat them with flour, shaking off the excess flour and setting the fillets aside. Continue until all fillets are coated with flour.

Melt butter in a 10- or 12-inch frying pan over medium heat. When pan is hot and butter melted, add fillets and cook until lightly browned; turn and brown on the other side. Fillets are most likely done at this point; check to see if the flesh is opaque rather than translucent in the middle and cook a little longer if not. Transfer fish to warmed serving plates. Splash vermouth into the pan, give a quick stir, cook 15 seconds, and pour equally over the plated fillets. Sprinkle with parsley and serve immediately. Excellent paired with crisp-tender broccoli or asparagus and warm, crusty bread. Serves 4.

Cook's Notes

- If any of the fillets are larger than you want to serve on one plate, lay them on your cutting board. Use a sharp boning knife or chef's knife to make an angled cut starting on top near the thickest end and cutting down toward the tail end to separate the fillet into 2 pieces, more or less equal in size. Visualize the resulting pieces before you cut and place your knife accordingly.

- ◆ For a crunchier coating, dredge fish in flour as above, dip in beaten egg, then dredge in unseasoned fine dried bread crumbs. Do the coating at the last minute; then cook as above.
- ◆ Variations? The world has zillions! Try adding 2 tablespoons capers to the butter and warming them and the parsley for a few seconds before pouring over fish. Or lightly brown in butter $1/2$ to $3/4$ cup sliced almonds and portion over fish—sole "almondine." Experiment!

BAKED RED SNAPPER

Fish baked in an herbed tomato sauce is a Mediterranean style of preparing fillets and steaks. Any piece of fish at least 1 inch thick will do, but very thin pieces of fish like sole fall apart and should be pan sautéed or broiled. A talented chef once told us that the secret to good seasoning is using just enough spice or herb that people will have to taste it more than once to determine what the flavor is. If they know at first bite, you have used too much. Remember, you can always add a little more seasoning, but you can't remove it once it is in the food. The ginger in this sauce is used this way—just enough to pique the flavor, but not overpower it.

1 pound red snapper fillets
Freshly squeezed juice of 1 lime
2 tablespoons olive oil
1 medium-size yellow onion (about 6 ounces), peeled and diced
2 cloves garlic, peeled and minced

1 can ($14^{1/2}$ ounces) peeled, diced tomatoes with liquid
$1/2$ cup minced fresh parsley
1 tablespoon minced fresh rosemary or 1 teaspoon dried rosemary
1 slice fresh ginger root (the size of a quarter), peeled and finely minced
1 teaspoon granulated sugar
Salt and freshly ground black pepper, to taste
1 teaspoon Worcestershire sauce
1 tablespoon freshly grated Parmesan cheese

To absorb any excess water in fish, place fillets on paper towels and squeeze gently. Pour the lime juice over fish and set aside.

Heat olive oil in a 10-inch frying pan over medium heat and add onion and garlic. Cook until onion is soft and translucent, about 4 minutes. Add tomatoes and remaining ingredients except fish. Cook, uncovered, over low heat until sauce is thick and smooth, about 15 minutes.

Meanwhile, preheat oven to 425°F. Place fish fillets in a single layer in an 11x7-inch baking dish. Pour sauce over fish and bake, uncovered, until fish flakes when pierced with fork, about 20 minutes. Serve from the baking dish.
Serves 4.

Cook's Notes

- ◆ **To serve 2 people, use $1/2$ pound of fillets and half the sauce in an 8x8-inch baking pan. Freeze the remaining sauce for another time.**

POACHED SALMON FILLETS OR STEAKS

Luckily for the beginning cook, poaching is the most foolproof (pardon the term!) method we can think of to cook fish. Poaching—cooking in simmering liquid—affords a moist cooking environment, requires no special equipment, and makes timing fairly predictable. If you are afflicted with Fear of Fish Cooking, gentle reader, start with poaching. It really isn't difficult, as you'll see. For information on the proper pans and other tips, see Cook's Notes. Poached salmon marries beautifully with simple steamed or boiled potatoes and a green vegetable. Cooled, it makes superb salad material.

4 fresh salmon steaks or fillets (4 to 8 ounces each)

1/2 stick (4 tablespoons) unsalted butter

1 lemon

Salt and freshly ground black pepper, to taste

1/4 cup chopped fresh parsley

Bring enough water to cover the thickest piece of fish by an inch to a boil in a pan in which all the fish pieces will fit at once, or use 2 pans simultaneously if necessary. Stand a ruler vertically next to the smallest piece of fish and note its thickness. Slide pieces of fish into the water, bring back to a gently bubbling simmer, and cook 10 minutes for each inch of thickness of the smallest piece. (For example, if your smallest steak is 1 inch thick, cook 10 minutes. If, say, you have a fillet piece that is only 3/4 inches thick, cook for 7 1/2 minutes.) While this method is not absolutely accurate, it beats any other formula we know about for simplicity.

While salmon is cooking, melt butter over low heat in a small saucepan. Cut lemon in half, squeeze 2 tablespoons of juice from one half and add to butter. Cut the other half into 4 wedges for garnish.

Test the smallest salmon piece for doneness—it should be opaque in the middle and register 120°F to 140°F on an instant-read thermometer, depending on how moist or dry you like your salmon. When done, gently lift the piece out of the water, slide onto a folded kitchen towel, and check the other pieces for doneness. Remove any skin still on the fish while it is warm—usually it will slide off easily.

Transfer fish to warmed serving plates, top with some of the lemon butter, sprinkle with a little salt, some freshly ground pepper, and some chopped parsley. Garnish with the wedges of lemon.
Serves 4.

Chilled Salmon with Mayonnaise

Omit the lemon butter. Serve lightly chilled with a little home-made mayonnaise, crusty bread, and marinated vegetables.

Cook's Notes

- **Picking a cooking vessel is the first step in poaching. Select a fairly shallow pan, with sides of 3 to 4 inches, large enough in diameter to fit the number of pieces you'll be cooking. A straight-sided 3- to 6-quart frying pan is a fine choice.**

- **Choose something with which to lift the fish out of the pan after cooking, such as a long metal turner/spatula.**
- **The cooking timing discussed here is approximate, since the shape of the pieces of fish affects their cooking rate. You'll want to check for doneness often while you get used to poaching.**
- **Many other types of fish respond well to poaching, as well. Try halibut, snapper, fresh tuna, and various kinds of sole.**

STEAMED CLAMS OR MUSSELS

We consider ourselves very lucky to live in the Pacific Northwest where fresh fish and seafood are abundant. But as we travel throughout the United States, we see that modern air transportation allows everyone access to this healthy eating alternative. This preparation of clams or mussels couldn't be easier or healthier. The mollusks are lean on their own and no additional fat is added. This can be a very quick first course or entrée with a nice loaf of crusty bread.

2 pounds fresh clams or mussels, in their shells

¾ cup dry white wine

1 clove garlic, peeled and finely chopped

1 shallot, peeled and finely chopped

2 sprigs fresh thyme

½ teaspoon salt or to taste

Freshly ground black pepper, to taste

1 teaspoon freshly squeezed lemon juice

Rinse clams or mussels under cold running water in a colander. Discard any that do not close after their rinse. If using mussels, trim the thickest part of their beards with a pair of kitchen shears or scissors. (Don't worry if a bit of the beards remains.) Put white wine, garlic, and shallot in a 4-quart saucepan or flameproof casserole fitted with a lid. Add leaves from the thyme sprigs to the pot; discard the twigs. Add salt, pepper, and clams or mussels to the pot. Bring to a boil, cover, and boil until the clams or mussels have opened, 4 to 8 minutes. Remove clams or mussels with a slotted spoon to a heated serving dish. Discard any that did not open.

Continue to boil the broth in the pot for an additional 3 to 4 minutes to reduce slightly. Add lemon juice and taste for seasoning. Add more salt or pepper, if necessary. Pour broth into individual ramekins. Using little cocktail or seafood forks, diners remove clams or mussels from their shells, dip them into the broth, and pop them happily into their mouths.

Serves 4 as an appetizer, 2 as a main course.

Cook's Notes

- **Shop around in your town for the best seafood dealer and learn to trust its staff. There is no middle ground for fish or seafood. It is either absolutely fresh or it is not!**
- **If possible, when buying clams or mussels for steaming, go for the smallest available. They generally seem sweeter.**

Spicy Seafood Stew >

Spicy Seafood Stew

Stews made with meat usually require long, slow cooking to tenderize the meat. Conversely, fish and shellfish are usually ruined by long cooking. This stew is a blend of vegetables and liquids to which you add your choice of fish and/or shellfish almost at the last minute! A combination of clam juice and chicken broth serves as a fine substitute for homemade fish stock. Your job as cook is to find honestly fresh fish and seafood. It should scarcely smell at all, and what odor there is should be faintly sweet rather than strongly fishy. The flesh should almost glisten, rather than looking dry around the edges. Full-flavored and firm-fleshed fish work best. Try albacore tuna, varieties of shark, salmon, marlin, swordfish, sturgeon, as well as halibut. We would avoid soft-textured soles, sablefish, and the like. Rock shrimp and scallops would be two fine choices for shellfish. The stew goes well with a crusty loaf of bread. Or serve over cooked rice or cooked small shell macaroni.

1 large yellow onion (10 to 12 ounces), peeled

1 rib celery, without leaves

1 medium carrot, peeled

1 clove garlic, peeled

2 fresh jalapeño chilies, split and seeded

2 tablespoons olive oil

1 bottle (7 to 8 ounces) clam juice

1 can (14½ ounces) low-sodium chicken broth

1½ cups water

1 tablespoon Worcestershire sauce

½ cup dry white wine

1 tablespoon tomato paste

1 teaspoon ground cumin

4 or 5 sprigs fresh thyme, tied with kitchen string

1 green bell pepper, halved, seeded, and deveined

Salt to taste (about 1 teaspoon)

Freshly ground black pepper, to taste

1 pound fish and/or shellfish (2 or 3 varieties) peeled or skinned and cut into 1-inch pieces

Green tops of 6 scallions, sliced

1 cup fresh oregano leaves, chopped

1 medium-size fresh tomato, peeled, seeded, and diced (page 46)

Finely chop ⅓ of the onion, celery, and carrot. Finely chop garlic and 1 of the jalapeños. In a 3- to 4-quart saucepan or straight-sided frying pan, heat olive oil over medium heat. Then add finely chopped vegetables and sauté until they are softened but not browned, about 5 minutes.

Add clam juice, chicken broth, the water, Worcestershire, wine, tomato paste, cumin, and thyme. Over high heat bring to a boil, reduce to a simmer, cover, and cook 5 minutes. Cut the bell pepper and remaining onion into large dice. Cut remaining celery and carrot into medium slices. Add these vegetables to the pan, cover, and cook another 8 to 10 minutes. Remove the thyme sprigs and taste the broth for salt, adding some if necessary. Add freshly ground black pepper to taste.

Finely chop remaining jalapeño. Stir fish and/or shellfish into broth and cook about 2 minutes. Add chopped jalapeño, scallions, oregano, and tomato.
Serves 6 to 8.

Cook's Notes

- ◆ 1 cup of oregano leaves is a lot, and may require 2 or 3 bunches. It is one of the primary flavors in the stew, so don't skimp!
- ◆ Some shark flesh looks beautifully fresh but at the same time smells slightly of ammonia. The smell goes away when the flesh is cooked.

BASIC DIRECTIONS FOR POACHED, SAUTÉED, AND GRILLED CHICKEN BREASTS

All the following instructions can be used to cook turkey breast, which is the same shape. Cooking time will be significantly longer, however, since the meat is much thicker.

Boning. Chicken breast is easier to cook uniformly if it has been boned. If a recipe calls for boneless breast and you have bone-in chicken, your first step is to pull the skin off the meat. Place the breast, bone side down, on your cutting board, then use a sharp boning knife to loosen the meat from the rib bones, starting at the "keel" bone on the thick side of the breast. Just keep the knife angled slightly toward the rib bones as you loosen the meat. Trim off any fat deposits from the boned meat and you are ready to cook. Boning a chicken breast is not hard to do and when you've done it several times, you'll have a skill you will not forget. Of course, you can always cheat and ask your butcher to do this for you.

Poaching. To poach a boneless breast, slip it into simmering water in a medium frying pan and bring the water back to a simmer. Cook until an instant-read thermometer registers 160°F, or the juices run clear, not red, when a knife is inserted into the thickest part of the meat. Start checking after 3 or 4 minutes. Remove breast with a slotted spoon and drain. If the chicken is to be cooled, slip it into cold water in a medium bowl for 10 minutes; then drain.

Sautéing. To sauté a boneless chicken breast, first flatten it a bit, which makes it easier to cook uniformly. Do this by placing the breast near the edge on a piece of plastic wrap. Fold plastic wrap over the top of the breast and smack the meat firmly several times with a flat (nonserrated) meat tenderizer, a small saucepan, anything flat and fairly heavy. Heat a frying pan over medium-high heat, add 2 to 4 tablespoons unsalted butter, olive oil, or vegetable oil, and add the chicken. Cook until lightly browned, turn, and brown on the second side, reducing heat to medium if necessary to prevent burning. Check for doneness (see poaching technique preceding) and if necessary continue to turn and cook. Allow about 5 minutes total cooking time.

Grilling. Prepare a charcoal fire or preheat a gas grill. Flatten boneless chicken breast as described above. Rub 1 or 2 teaspoons of olive oil or vegetable oil over the meat, and place on the grill's cooking grid. Turn when the edges of the breast are turning white and drying a bit. Cook until done (as described under poaching), always leaving the grill covered by a ventilated lid if it is so equipped in order to trap as much flavorful smoke as possible. Allow about 6 minutes total cooking time.

Roast Chicken

Roasting a chicken is so easy to do that it ought to be against the law! If you can fall out of bed, you've got the brains to do this. So pay attention. All you really need is an oven that works, an ovenproof baking pan, a roasting rack that fits the pan and—ideally—an instant-read thermometer. OK, for a more professional look you can rustle up a little white kitchen string and truss the hapless bird so it looks like it came from some snooty "gourmet" restaurant, but it is not required. The bird roasts just as well in—how do we say this—a "relaxed" position. A properly roasted chicken is wonderfully moist and goes with all manner of accompaniments plain or fancy, such as corn on the cob, baked or parslied potatoes, sautéed carrots, or steamed green beans. Leftover roasted chicken is worth killing for!

1 fresh chicken (2½ to 5 pounds)
Salt and freshly ground black pepper, to taste

Preheat oven to 400°F. Liberate the fowl from its plastic bag if it came so clothed. Remove the bag of giblets (all of which were once vital to the bird's well-being) from the cavity. (See Cook's Notes for ideas on using them.) Pull out any large fat deposits from the cavity. Trim any loose skin with a sharp knife. Removing the tail is optional—some people think it looks cute.

Place a roasting rack in a baking pan with sides at least 1 inch high. (We often use one of those 9x13-inch glass baking pans that accommodate an adjustable V-shaped roast rack.) Set the bird on the rack breast side up. Grind a little fresh pepper onto it and sprinkle lightly with salt. Adding a little salt in the cavity is optional; some cooks do, some don't.

Place the baking pan on a rack in the lower-middle section of the oven. Roast until the juices run clear when a sharp knife is inserted into the joint between the body and thigh, or when your instant-read thermometer registers 170°F testing the same joint, 45 to 60 minutes. Remove chicken from the oven, cover loosely with aluminum foil, and allow to rest for 10 minutes before you carve. This rest allows the juices to "set," resulting in a moister chicken and less juice loss on your carving board.

You don't have to be a brain surgeon to carve a roast chicken, but you do need a sharp knife (a chef's knife works if you don't own a carving knife). With the bird sitting breast side up on your cutting board, cut down between the thigh and the body until you feel bone; use your hands or a carving fork to twist the leg/thigh away from the body so you can see the joint. Just cut through the joint and you've got a leg/thigh ready to serve. Repeat on the other side of the bird. If you want to serve the wings separately, use the same technique, cutting into the "armpit" under the wing to find the joint. Twist the wing out and cut through the joint. To carve the breast meat off the body of the bird, make a cut along each side of the "keel" bone running along the top of the breast. Angle your knife slightly toward the rib cage while you loosen the meat by moving your knife back and forth down the side of the chicken. Use the tip of the knife to cut the meat away from the diagonal wishbone at the wide end of the bird; each half-breast piece of meat should come off the chicken pretty much in one piece. What remains is the rib cage and back of the chicken. Pick the carcass later for fine leftover meat for soups or salads.

Serves 4.

Cook's Notes

◆ **Rub bird with a mixture of 1 tablespoon Dijon-style mustard and 1 tablespoon olive oil.**

◆ **Cut a lemon in half, squeeze and save the juice, and place lemon halves in the cavity along with a crushed garlic clove. Brush the lemon juice over the chicken every 15 minutes during roasting.**

◆ **Place some fresh herb sprigs in the cavity. Sprinkle some chopped fresh herbs over the outside of the chicken as it roasts.**

◆ **Hearts, gizzards, and necks are excellent homemade stock materials—freeze them for later use; the liver (if present) is best not used in stock, so refrigerate it and plan to use within 3 or 4 days in another meal.**

A Note of Caution When Handling Poultry

Salmonella bacteria are usually present in raw poultry, so cutting boards, knives, and other utensils that have been used to prepare raw poultry should be washed with hot, soapy water or run through your dishwasher before being used to prepare uncooked foods like salads. Wash your hands thoroughly after handling raw poultry before handling food that will not be cooked.

BRAISED CHICKEN THIGHS

This recipe is for you dark-meat lovers out there. You can buy thighs with the bone in and remove the skin, or buy boneless, skinless ones. These are easier to serve and eat, but if you like gnawing on the bone like we do, removing the skin is easy. We take the skin off because it contains so much fat and cholesterol—even though it is the best-tasting part. Buy the most inexpensive bottle of sherry for use in cooking, but don't buy a product called "cooking sherry"—we do not recommend it. Use a dry (fino) or medium (amontillado), but not a sweet sherry. This recipe is quick and simple, and can be doubled easily for company.

4 chicken thighs, skin removed
$\frac{1}{4}$ cup all-purpose flour
1 teaspoon salt
1 teaspoon dried sage
1 teaspoon dried thyme
$\frac{1}{2}$ teaspoon paprika
1 tablespoon olive oil
1 tablespoon unsalted butter
$\frac{1}{2}$ cup peeled and finely diced yellow onion
$\frac{1}{4}$ pound fresh mushrooms, thinly sliced
$\frac{1}{4}$ cup sherry

Dry chicken pieces with paper towels so the flour will stick to them. Mix flour with salt, sage, thyme, and paprika in a plastic bag, add chicken, and close tightly. Shake well so chicken thighs are coated.

Heat oil and butter together over medium heat in a 10-inch frying pan until the butter foams. Brown thighs on both sides and remove to a dish. Add onions and mushrooms to the pan and sauté until onions are translucent, about 5 minutes. Return chicken to pan and add sherry.

Cook for 2 to 3 minutes, turn heat to low, cover, and simmer until juices run clear when chicken is pricked with a fork near the bone, about 25 minutes.
Serves 2 to 4.

Cook's Notes

◆   **If you are not concerned about cholesterol and like to eat the skin of the chicken, by all means leave it on. Salt and freshly ground black pepper can be added, but poultry seasoning is quite flavorful and has some salt in it, so taste first.**

CHICKEN STIR-FRY

You don't need remarkable skill to succeed in stir-frying, just a little patience and a sharp knife! Most of the work is done in advance of the cooking, sadly devoid of any glamour. So give your knife or slicing cleaver a few swipes on the sharpening steel and get out the cutting board, because that is where the action starts. This simple but tasty stir-fry is fine accompanied with cooked rice or noodles—hot or at room temperature, plain or tossed with a little sesame oil. Believe us—it's also good with a baked potato.

6 scallions

2 cloves garlic, peeled

2 slices unpeeled fresh ginger root (about the size of a quarter)

1 red bell pepper, seeded, deveined, and cut into ½-inch dice

1 medium zucchini

½ cup plus 3 tablespoons low-sodium chicken broth

2½ tablespooons good-quality light soy sauce

2 tablespoons dry sherry

1½ teaspoons unseasoned rice vinegar

1½ teaspoons granulated sugar

1½ teaspoons Asian sesame oil

1 pound boneless, skinless chicken breast or thigh,
     cut into ½-inch dice

2 tablespoons cornstarch

¼ cup corn oil

Slice green scallion tops and set aside on a small plate. Mince white part of scallions, garlic, and ginger and set aside in a small bowl. Cut zucchini in half lengthwise, then cut into ¼-inch slices. In a small bowl, combine ½ cup of the chicken broth, soy sauce, sherry, rice vinegar, sugar, and sesame oil. Place cornstarch and the 3 tablespoons chicken broth in a small jar and cover with a tight-fitting lid.

Heat a 12- to 14-inch wok or large sauté pan over medium-high heat until you can feel the heat from the pan. Swirl in corn oil, heat 10 seconds, then add minced scallions, garlic, and ginger. Stir almost constantly, with a wooden spoon or wok spatula, until the garlic just begins to color a bit. Toss in bell pepper and stir-fry for 1 to 2 minutes until its color brightens. Add zucchini and chicken broth mixture. Bring to a boil and add chicken pieces. Cook for 1 minute, stirring occasionally, bringing sauce back to a boil. Give the cornstarch mixture a shake to combine well, then pour a little at a time into the chicken mixture while you stir, stopping when you have thickened but not solidified the sauce! (It will thicken a bit more as it cools.) Stir in scallion tops and pour into a warmed serving dish.

Serves 4.

Cook's Notes

- All manner of other vegetables could be added. Instead of zucchini, try broccoli or cauliflower florets, slices of bok choy, carrot slices, snow peas, sugar snap peas, and so forth. Cook until vegetable is just crisp-tender, then add chicken and continue the recipe.
- For a spicy dish add 1 teaspoon Chinese chili paste or hot chili oil.
- Add ¼ cup minced fresh cilantro leaves with the scallion tops.

BUTTERFLIED ROASTED CORNISH GAME HENS

These cute little birds make a simple and elegant entrée for entertaining. Some butchers offer them fresh, but most often you will find game hens in the frozen section of the supermarket. Just plan a couple of days before serving so that you can slowly defrost them in the refrigerator. We prefer to use an imported Emmenthaler cheese in this recipe, but a good-quality domestic Swiss is fine, as well.

4 Rock Cornish game hens

¼ cup Dijon-style mustard

1 tablespoon finely chopped fresh rosemary

Salt and freshly ground black pepper, to taste

Vegetable oil, for brushing birds

½ cup fine, dry bread crumbs

¼ cup finely shredded Swiss cheese (about 1 ounce)

Remove the giblet package from each of the birds. (Save the livers to sauté for another meal, and save the necks for making stock.) Rinse birds and dry them well. To butterfly the birds, cut along each side of the backbone with poultry shears or good all-purpose kitchen shears and remove the backbone. (Save it for making stock.) Sorry, that cute little tail has to go, too. Flatten the birds slightly and place them, breast side up, on a baking sheet covered with aluminum foil. (If you have a flat roasting rack place it on the lined pan and position the birds on the rack.)

Preheat broiler and set the broiling rack about 6 inches below it. (If oven is separate from your broiler, preheat oven to 375°F.) In a measuring cup, mix mustard, rosemary, salt, and pepper.

Spread a little vegetable oil over the birds and place under the broiler until birds are lightly browned, about 6 minutes. Remove from the oven and spread with the mustard mixture, dividing as evenly as possible; sprinkle with dry bread crumbs. Place birds back under the broiler just until the crumbs start to brown, about 1 minute. Remove the birds from the broiler.

Turn down oven to 375°F. Sprinkle birds with shredded cheese. Place them back in the oven and bake until an instant-read thermometer registers 170°F when inserted in the thigh, 20 to 25 minutes. Remove from oven and let the birds rest for about 5 minutes before placing on warm plates to serve. Serves 4.

ROAST TURKEY AND DRESSING

The wild turkey, instead of the eagle, almost became our national bird, and maybe in some ways it is. Many Americans view their Thanksgiving bird as essential to the holiday. But we really encourage you to think of the fine turkey at other times of the year as well. Turkey meat is certainly in keeping with the demands of our modern diet—lean and inexpensive. We have offered a dressing recipe that is fairly classic, with one exception; the dressing is cooked outside the turkey in a separate baking pan. This is really a safer method of cooking. (Sometimes with a big bird the dressing stays at a mildly warm temperature for too long before reaching an oven heat high enough to kill bacteria.) Besides, it really is easier to cook the dressing separately as it can be prepared a day in advance and refrigerated. (Even if stuffing the dressing inside the bird, this should never be done until the very last minute.) If you are using a frozen turkey, it should be defrosted in the refrigerator (never at room temperature) for 3 to 4 days.

1 turkey (12 to 14 pounds)
Olive oil, for brushing turkey
Salt and freshly ground black pepper, to taste

< Butterflied Roasted Cornish Game Hens

Dressing

9 cups day-old bread cubes, cut into 1/2-inch-square cubes
    (about 1 medium-size French loaf or sandwich loaf)
1/2 stick (4 tablespoons) unsalted butter; plus more butter, at room
    temperature, for the baking pan
1 large yellow onion (about 8 ounces), peeled and coarsely chopped
2 large ribs celery, trimmed and coarsely chopped
1/4 teaspoon celery seed
2 large eggs, lightly beaten
3 cups Chicken Stock (page 32) or canned low-sodium chicken broth
1 teaspoon salt
Freshly ground black pepper, to taste
1/2 cup chopped pecans

Gravy

Giblets from turkey (neck, gizzard, liver, heart, and tail)
2 tablespoons unsalted butter
3 cups Chicken Stock (page 32) or canned low-sodium chicken broth
6 whole black peppercorns
1 medium-size yellow onion (about 6 ounces), peeled and
    finely chopped
2 tablespoons all-purpose flour
Pan drippings from turkey
Salt, if needed

Preheat oven to 350°F. Remove turkey from its wrap. Remove neck and giblets from inside the cavity and set aside to make the gravy. Rinse bird completely inside and out. Pat dry with paper towels. Position one oven rack at the lowest level in the oven and the other rack just above it. Place bird on a roasting rack, breast side up, in a roasting pan with sides. With your hands, thoroughly rub the outside of the bird with olive oil. Sprinkle a bit of salt and pepper over the outside of the bird and in its cavity. Place bird in the oven and roast until an instant-read thermometer registers 160°F when pierced into the thickest point of the thigh, 1¾ to 2 hours. Plan to let the bird rest for about 15 minutes before carving to let the juices set. While turkey is roasting, prepare dressing and gravy.

To make the dressing

Place bread cubes in a large mixing bowl. Melt butter in a 10-inch frying pan over medium heat. Add the chopped celery and onion and cook until wilted, but not brown, about 3 to 4 minutes. Add onion-celery mixture to bread cubes. Then add remaining ingredients and toss well with your hands or a large mixing spoon. Butter a 9x13-inch baking dish. Place stuffing in dish and cover with aluminum foil.

About 20 minutes before the turkey is done, place the covered dish of stuffing in the oven and bake for 20 minutes. When you remove the turkey from the oven, increase the oven temperature to 400°F and uncover the dressing. Bake until nicely brown and crisp on top, about 20 minutes.

To make the gravy

Rinse turkey giblets and dry completely with paper towels. Melt 1 tablespoon of the butter in an 8-inch frying pan over medium-high heat. When hot, add all giblets and brown well on both sides. In the meantime, combine stock and peppercorns in a 3-quart saucepan. Bring to a boil, reduce heat to simmer. Add browned giblets (*except liver*) to the simmering stock and cook until tender, about 40 minutes. Set aside liver. With a slotted spoon remove neck and giblets from stock and allow them to cool.

In the meantime, add the remaining tablespoon butter to the frying pan, melt over medium heat, and add chopped onion. Cook until onion is well browned, about 10 minutes. Sprinkle flour over onion and continue cooking, about 3 more minutes. With a ladle dip some of the hot stock out of the saucepan and, with a whisk, blend it into onion mixture. Gradually add 2 more ladles of hot stock, continuing to whisk all the while. This mixture should thicken like a loose paste. Add this mixture back into the saucepan and continue to stir frequently over low heat until gravy has thickened, 5 to 8 minutes.

Strain pan drippings from the turkey into a cup or a gravy strainer. Allow to set for a few moments for the fat to rise to the surface, and then strain as much of the fat off as your conscience dictates. (Fat does add flavor.) Taste the gravy at this point for salt. We have found no salt is needed when using canned stock. Shred meat from the neck of the turkey, and cut liver, heart, and gizzard into small dice. Add to gravy. Allow to warm completely before serving. *Serves 6.*

Cook's Notes

- **The dressing can be prepared and even baked a day in advance. To rewarm, remove from the refrigerator about 1½ hours before serving time. Then place in a preheated 350°F oven for about 20 minutes.**
- **The gravy can also be prepared in part a day in advance of serving. Place in a glass bowl covered with plstic wrap and**

store in refrigerator. Add pan drippings to the gravy and then warm in a saucepan just before serving.

- Not everyone likes celery seed. Instead use 1 tablespoon chopped fresh sage or thyme in the dressing. You also can add either herb in addition to the celery seed, if desired.
- For carving instructions for the big bird, see how to do it on a littler bird in the Roast Chicken recipe (page 116).

CURRIED TURKEY OR CHICKEN

What to do with Thanksgiving turkey leftovers? After two days of eating roast turkey we are ready for a change. Turning the leftovers into a curry with aromatic spices, coconut, dried apricots, and peas makes for a wonderful change of flavors. If you are planning to cook Roast Chicken (page 116) one night, buy an extra chicken, roast two, and use the second one to make a curry later in the week. This dish is great for company. All the cooking is done ahead and the curry is ready to serve when you are. Having little bowls of condiments on the table for passing makes this recipe even more fun. Serve with steamed rice or pilaf. This recipe can be cut in half for a smaller group.

3 tablespoons vegetable oil

2 yellow onions (about 1 pound total), peeled and cut into
    thin wedges

2 cloves garlic, peeled and minced

2 slices fresh ginger root (about the size of a quarter), minced

1 1/2 teaspoons ground coriander

1 1/2 teaspoons ground cumin

1 teaspoon ground turmeric

2 whole cloves

2-inch piece cinnamon stick

1 teaspoon salt

1/4 teaspoon cayenne pepper

1 tablespoon all-purpose flour

1 1/2 cups Chicken Stock (page 32) or canned low-sodium
    chicken broth

1/4 cup good-quality shredded coconut (preferably unsweetened)

12 dried apricots, cut into quarters

8 cups cubed roasted turkey or chicken

1 cup frozen peas

2 cups plain low-fat yogurt

6 to 8 cups cooked long-grain white rice (page 75)

Condiments

1/2 cup toasted good-quality shredded coconut
    (preferably unsweetened), following

1 cup toasted unsalted cashews or peanuts, following

1/2 cup mango chutney or other fruit chutney

1 cup diced fresh pineapple

1/4 cup thinly sliced scallions, include green part

Heat a 6-quart straight-sided frying pan over medium-high heat and add oil. When hot add onions, garlic, and ginger. Sauté, stirring frequently, until onions are soft and lightly golden, about 10 minutes. Add coriander, cumin, turmeric, cloves, cinnamon, salt, and cayenne. Sauté, stirring often, an additional 5 minutes.

Sprinkle flour over onions in pan and stir to combine. Gradually stir in stock, then add coconut and apricots. Bring mixture to a simmer, reduce heat to maintain a slow simmer, cover, and cook an additional 15 minutes. Add turkey or chicken and cook, covered, 10 minutes more. Remove from heat and keep covered until ready to serve. Just before serving, bring mixture back to a simmer, stir in peas and yogurt, and heat through. Serve over cooked rice. Pass bowls of condiments at the table.

Serves 6 to 8.

Toasted Coconut and Nuts

To toast coconut, heat a dry, heavy-bottomed frying pan over medium heat. Add coconut to pan and cook, stirring constantly, until lightly browned. Remove to a plate to cool. Add cashews or peanuts to the hot pan and cook, stirring occasionally, until lightly browned; remove to a plate to cool. Alternatively, nuts can be browned in a microwave. Place in a single layer on a plate, microwave on high power for 2 to 3 minutes, watching carefully that they don't burn.

ROAST DUCK WITH APPLE-ONION SAUTÉ

We have found a perfectly wonderful way to roast a duck. It is simple and it accomplishes two important elements. First, the long roasting allows for an almost complete rendering of fat, making the duck meat tender, but not tummy-churning rich. Second, a finish under the broiler gives a crisp, tasty skin. Most ducks these days are found in the freezer section of your supermarket, so plan your purchase three or four days in advance to allow for a slow defrost in the refrigerator. We have embellished the recipe with a simple little sauté for some color and textural contrast. Fruit flavors always marry well with duck.

> 1 duck (about 5 pounds)
> Salt and freshly ground black pepper, to taste
> 2 tablespoons unsalted butter
> ½ cup Chicken Stock (page 32) or canned low-sodium chicken broth

Apple-Onion Sauté

> 1 medium-size yellow onion (about 8 ounces), peeled and thinly sliced
> 1 medium tart green apple, peeled, seeded, and thinly sliced
> ½ teaspoon salt
> Freshly ground black pepper, to taste
> 1 teaspoon fresh thyme leaves
> ½ cup dried cranberries or dried cherries

Preheat oven to 350°F. Remove neck and giblets from the cavity of the duck. (Save these—except liver—for making stock). Rinse duck thoroughly inside and out and dry with paper towels. With a paring knife cut away visible large pieces of fat around the opening to the cavity. Sprinkle duck lightly with salt and pepper, inside and out.

In a 12-inch frying pan, melt butter over medium heat. Add duck and brown on all sides, 2 to 3 minutes per side. Transfer duck to a rack placed in a roasting pan with sides at least 1 inch deep. Place in the oven and roast for 2½ hours. Baste the bird with chicken stock about every ½ hour.

Remove all but about 2 tablespoons of fat from the pan used to brown the duck. Heat fat until hot and add onions. Cook slowly over medium-low to low heat until onions are very tender and nicely browned, 15 to 20 minutes. Add apple slices and continue to cook until apples are soft, about 10 more minutes. Add salt, pepper, thyme, and cranberries and sauté to blend the flavors, about 2 more minutes. Turn off heat and set mixture aside until the duck is done.

Remove duck from oven and preheat the broiler. Add about 2 tablespoons of any remaining chicken stock or water to the apple-onion mixture and place over low heat. Place duck about 6 inches under the broiler to brown and crisp the skin. Watch closely; brown is what we are aiming for, not charred. Remove duck to a carving board and carve as directed for Roast Chicken (page 116). Serve each portion of duck with a spoonful of the apple-onion mixture.
Serves 2 or 3.

Cook's Notes

- **If you are not able to find either dried cranberries or dried cherries, use dark or golden raisins. The mixture will be a little sweeter and less tart, but still yummy.**
- **Ducks really do not have a lot of meat on them; that's why we specify a 5-pound duck to feed 2 or 3 people. If you have lots of other items on the dinner table, you may stretch it to serve 4, but if you have the oven space, you may want to roast 2 ducks. Any leftovers are heavenly.**

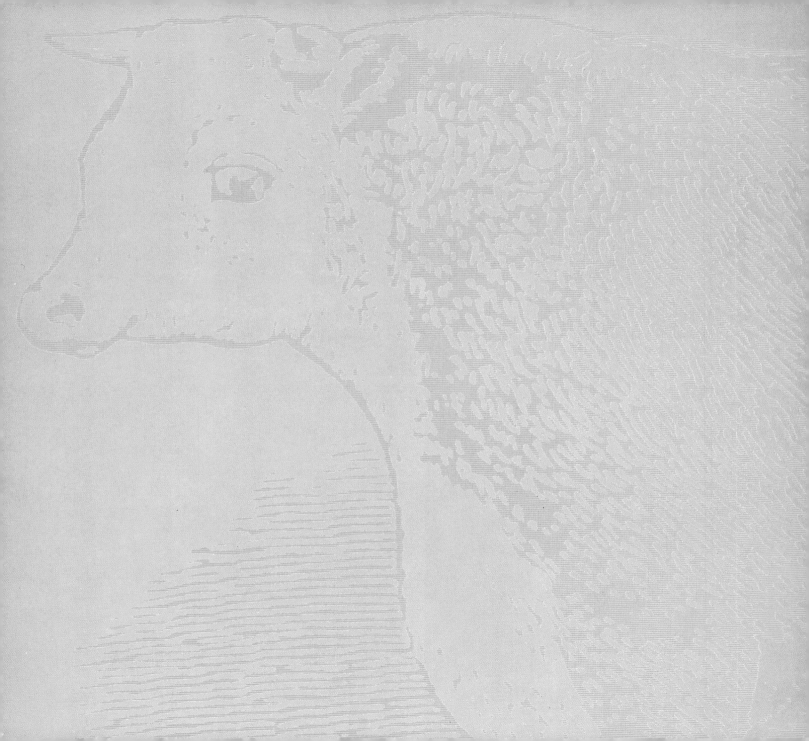

MEATS

*Old-fashioned ways with beef, pork, and lamb—comfort foods,
mostly braised or baked*

How to Grill and Panfry Steaks and Burgers

Panfrying

Panfrying (not "sautéing," because no fat is added to the pan) is surely the world's simplest means of cooking a steak or hamburger patty. Select a heavy-bottomed frying pan big enough for the job and heat it over medium-high heat until you can feel heat from the metal. (You can use a nonstick pan if you like, but high-heat cooking like panfrying shortens the life of many kinds of nonstick pans.) Turn on the kitchen exhaust fan if you have one. Place steaks or burgers in the pan and season with a pinch of salt and some freshly ground black pepper. Do not try to move them for 2 or 3 minutes; a crust will form in that time, making it easier to turn the meat. Use a sturdy metal spatula to turn the meat; then brown and season the other side. Turn the heat down to medium, if necessary, to prevent burning before the meat is cooked to your liking.

Testing for doneness. Use an instant-read thermometer to gauge doneness in the center of meat: 110°F to 120°F if you like yours warm and red in the center (medium rare); 130°F to 140°F, for warm and pink (medium); or higher if you prefer your meat well done. Or, make a discreet cut into the center of the meat with a small sharp knife and look at the color—you'll lose more juice this way, but it's better than nothing.

< Beef Stew

Panfrying tip. There is a round, screenlike device with a handle called a spatter-screen or spatter-shield that can be placed over a pan during panfrying and sautéing. It lets steam evaporate but traps most of the tiny fat droplets which otherwise spatter all over your cooktop during these cooking operations. It is inexpensive and useful.

Grilling

To grill steaks or burgers, first start a charcoal fire and let it burn until the coals are covered in a white ash before spreading the coals. A chimney-style starter device is the fastest method and avoids the need to use charcoal starter fluid—look for one anywhere quality grilling equipment is sold. Or, preheat your gas grill. Place the steaks or burgers on the cooking grid, season them with salt and freshly ground black pepper, and cook (covered with the ventilated lid if so equipped) until they are nicely browned on one side. Turn, season, and cook on the other side until done to your liking. (See "Testing for doneness" above.) Grilling with the lid on (but vent holes open) gives by far the best flavor, trapping much more of the flavorful smoke produced by fats and juices dripping onto hot coals or lava rocks.

Meat Loaf

This is a classic meat loaf, easy to prepare without a lot of fuss. It's great served right away, or it can be made ahead and reheated. Thinly sliced and paired with hearty bread, meat loaf makes a terrific sandwich.

Ground meats tend to lose moisture when frozen, so freezing cooked meat loaf or leftovers can be done, but for quality's sake is not recommended. Accompany with your favorite condiment (ketchup is the classic choice). Mashed potatoes are almost a must here, but home fries aren't bad either. Add a nice green vegetable, such as steamed green beans or broccoli, and you're in business.

6 slices white or whole wheat bread

$^1/_2$ cup dry red wine or water

$1^1/_2$ pounds very lean ground beef (about 9 percent fat)

$^1/_4$ pound ground pork or an additional $^1/_4$ pound ground beef

$^1/_4$ pound mild or hot bulk Italian sausage (see Cook's Notes)

1 medium-size yellow onion (about 5 ounces), peeled, cut in half, and grated

$^1/_2$ bunch fresh parsley, minced

3 tablespoons minced fresh basil or $1^1/_2$ tablespoons dried basil

1 extra-large egg, lightly beaten

2 teaspoons salt

$^1/_2$ teaspoon freshly ground black pepper

Preheat oven to 375°F. Place bread in a medium-size bowl and pour wine or water over it. Let stand for 10 minutes, then squeeze dry with your hands and set aside, retaining liquid that remains.

In a large bowl, combine ground meats, then add bread with soaking liquid and all remaining ingredients. Blend thoroughly, kneading with your hands to make sure there are no chunks of bread visible. With dampened hands shape into a 6x10-inch oblong loaf and place in a 9x13-inch baking pan. Rub the meat loaf with about $^1/_4$ cup of water to make it smooth; this also gives it some additional moisture while baking.

Bake meat loaf, uncovered, until an instant-read thermometer inserted in the center registers 150°F, about 1 hour. (The meat will continue to cook out of the oven.)

Remove meat loaf from oven and allow to rest for 5 to 10 minutes before slicing and serving. This allows the meat to firm up and the internal juices to stay within the loaf. Slice into $^3/_4$-inch slices and serve.
Serves 8.

Cook's Notes

◆   Bulk Italian sausage is uncooked sausage that is sold without being stuffed into casings. If you can't find Italian sausage sold in bulk, then buy the links and remove the meat from casings before cooking.

POT ROAST

Pot roast is often preceded by the term "old-fashioned"—rightfully. For many of us, pot roast conjures up memories of grandmother's house and family Sunday dinners. The vegetables are cooked with the meat and served as a colorful wreath surrounding it on the platter. We've used a 4-pound roast, which will serve company or you can feast on leftovers for several meals (the flavor improves overnight). Beef for pot roast is called by several names: blade-cut chuck roast, cross rib roast, rump roast, sirloin tip roast, or even "pot roast." Any of these will work. The meat should have some marbling of fat so it will be tender. But you should trim most of the excess visible fat from the outside; otherwise your drippings will be too greasy. *We recommend using a utensil called a "gravy strainer" to remove excess fat from the drippings before you serve them at the table.*

1/2 cup all-purpose flour

2 teaspoons salt

1 1/2 teaspoons freshly ground black pepper

4-pound boneless beef roast, trimmed of excess fat

2 tablespoons olive oil

1 tablespoon unsalted butter

1 medium-size yellow onion (5 ounces), peeled and thinly sliced

3 ribs celery with leaves, sliced

1/2 cup dry red wine or canned beef broth

1 1/2 pounds small red potatoes, unpeeled except for a strip
    peeled around the middle

1/2 pound baby carrots, peeled, or 4 regular carrots,
    peeled and cut into 2-inch pieces

1 pound small whole boiling onions, peeled, or 1 package
    (20 ounces) frozen whole baby onions

1 tablespoon cornstarch (optional)

1/2 cup minced fresh parsley

Place flour, salt, and pepper in a shallow dish and dredge the roast to coat on all sides. Heat olive oil and butter over medium-high heat in a heavy 6-quart saucepan or flame-proof casserole until butter foams. Add meat and brown on all sides, then remove to a large plate. In the same pan, sauté onion and celery over medium heat until onion is translucent, about 5 minutes; add to meat on plate. Add wine to pan and deglaze by scraping the browned bits from the bottom. Return meat and onion-celery mixture to pan and cook over medium heat briefly to reduce the volume of the wine, 3 to 4 minutes.

Reduce heat to low, cover pan, and simmer until meat begins to feel tender when pierced with a fork, about 2 hours. Add potatoes, carrots, and onions around and over meat. Cover again and continue cooking until meat is very tender and vegetables are cooked, 1 to 1 1/2 hours. (If the vegetables are done and the meat needs a little more time, remove them to a dish and add them back at the end to reheat.)

Remove meat to a large platter and allow to stand 10 minutes before slicing. Remove vegetables with a slotted spoon to a bowl and keep warm. Skim excess fat from top of drippings with a spoon or paper towels, or use a gravy strainer to remove fat. If you prefer a thicker gravy, mix 1 tablespoon cornstarch with 1 tablespoon water to make a paste and stir it into the gravy, cooking until it thickens, about 2 or 3 minutes. Slice meat and place in the middle of the serving platter; arrange the vegetables around it. Garnish with the minced parsley. Pass the gravy in a bowl at the table. *Serves 8 to 10.*

Cook's Notes

- **You can use any seasonings you like in the flour mixture for dredging the meat—dried herbs such as oregano, thyme, etc. work especially well, but seasoned salts or pepper also add an interesting flavor.**
- **Leftover pot roast can be used for cold sandwiches or for hot beef sandwiches with some of the gravy. It is also great in any casserole that calls for cooked meat.**

- To reduce the recipe buy a roast that weighs 2 to 3 pounds and use a lesser amount of vegetables.
- Add 1 can (14½ ounces) peeled, diced tomatoes with liquid and a bay leaf to the cooking liquid. Remove bay leaf before serving.

BEEF STEW

Braising is a method of cooking meat with a little liquid, as opposed to boiling. Stews and pot roasts are braised, which keeps them moist and tender. We recommend that you buy a piece of chuck and cut it into cubes. Chuck is fattier than other cuts and meat that is too lean will take very long to cook and may never get really tender. This is a delicious one-pot meal, served with good bread for dunking and a green salad. It is also a great opportunity to use a pretty Dutch oven for cooking and serving the stew at the table right from the pot.

½ cup all-purpose flour

1 teaspoon salt

½ teaspoon freshly ground black pepper

⅛ teaspoon ground allspice

1¼ pounds beef chuck, cut into 1½-inch cubes

¼ cup olive oil or vegetable oil

1 medium-size yellow onion (about 5 ounces), peeled and diced

1 rib celery with leaves, sliced

½ cup dry red wine

1 can (14 ounces) beef broth

2 cloves garlic, peeled and pressed

1 teaspoon grated orange zest

2 teaspoons dried thyme

2 teaspoons dried oregano

½ cup minced fresh parsley

10 small red potatoes, unpeeled except for a strip around the middle

2 large carrots, peeled and cut into ½ inch pieces, or

⅓⁄₂ pound whole baby carrots

1 package (10 ounces) frozen whole baby onions, thawed

In a measuring cup, mix flour with salt, pepper, and allspice. Place in a zippered plastic bag, add beef, seal shut, and shake to coat meat completely. Remove meat and reserve seasoned flour for thickening gravy. Heat oil in a 6-quart saucepan or flameproof casserole over medium heat. Brown meat on all sides and remove to a plate. Add onion and celery to pan and cook until onion is translucent, about 5 minutes. Remove from pan and place with meat.

Add wine to pot and deglaze by scraping any browned bits from the bottom. Add beef broth gradually; then return meat, onion, and celery to pan. Add garlic, orange zest, thyme, oregano, and ¼ cup of the minced parsley. Cover and cook over medium to low heat until the meat begins to feel tender when pierced with a fork, 1½ to 2 hours. Stir occasionally to prevent sticking. After 1 hour add the potatoes, carrots, and baby onions to the stew. Continue cooking until the meat and vegetables are tender when pierced with a fork, 45 minutes to 1 hour longer. If gravy is too thin, mix reserved flour with a little water to make a paste and gradually stir into pan until thickened to your taste. Serve directly from the cooking pan or in a large serving bowl. Garnish with the remaining minced parsley.

Serves 4 to 6.

- If you can't find small red potatoes, buy larger ones, and quarter them so they are close to the size of the carrots. You will need about 6 larger potatoes.
- Many markets now carry baby carrots in cellophane bags. They are great for this dish.
- Using a large (½ gallon) zippered plastic bag is a very efficient way to dredge meat in the seasoned flour without making a mess in the kitchen or dirtying extra dishes. Keep the flour mixture that remains in case you need it to add at the end because your stew is too watery.

PRIME RIB OF BEEF

What does it take to make a perfect prime rib of beef? Basically, a good butcher, an accurate meat thermometer, and timing. Prime rib (also called standing rib roast of beef) is dinner party fare or holiday entertaining at its best. We think of serving prime rib at Christmas, New Year's Eve, or even at Easter. It is an expensive piece of meat and usually cut to serve five to six at a minimum. However, for the beginning cook, roasting a prime rib offers great results for a modest amount of labor. Serve the garlic-rubbed prime rib with roasted potatoes or scalloped potatoes. Prime rib is such a classic, we think traditional accompaniments suit it best. Once the roast is in the oven, you'll have time to prepare a salad and vegetable, and maybe even relax with a glass of wine before dinner is served.

1 standing rib roast of beef (5 to 6 pounds)

7 large cloves garlic, peeled

2 teaspoons salt

Preheat oven to 450°F. Place meat, bone side down, in roasting pan, or on a heavy baking sheet with at least 1-inch sides. Make a paste of the garlic and salt, using a food processor, garlic press, or mortar and pestle (see Cook's Notes). Spread garlic paste evenly over the top and sides of roast. Place in oven for 30 minutes, then reduce temperature to 300°F.

After one hour of roasting at 300°F, check temperature of roast. Insert an instant-read thermometer into the center of roast, away from any bone or fat pockets. For a rare roast, 120°F is the temperature you are looking for, medium is 130°F to 135°F, and well-done is closer to 150°F. Depending on the temperature reading, either cook the roast longer, checking every 10 minutes, or remove roast from oven.

When the roast is done, cover it loosely with foil and allow to rest for 20 minutes before carving. This keeps the juices in the meat, instead of all over the carving board. Carve the roast to the thickness you desire, using a very sharp knife. Serve either with the bone or without.

Cook's Notes

- A little planning will be required to have your entrée done at the same time. Plan backwards from the time you want to serve dinner. If dinner is to be at 7:00 p.m., you'll want the roast to come out of the oven at 6:40 p.m.

Allowing about 2 hours for actual cooking time, the roast should be ready to go into the oven at 4:40 p.m. Give yourself 30 minutes of preparation time, so head into the kitchen by 4:10 p.m. This schedule is just a guideline; it is how an experienced cook would think about planning this type of dinner. Don't work by a stopwatch; relax and have fun.

- ◆ A porcelain mortar and pestle is what pharmacists once used to pulverize pills. It is a wonderful tool for this task and also for grinding spices. Though not necessarily in a beginning cook's arsenal, it is handy.
- ◆ Always wash your meat thermometer after testing the roast each time. Bacteria from the meat form on the stem if the thermometer is just left on the counter between testings; then reinserting the unwashed thermometer results in bacteria being injected into the meat.
- ◆ If you don't like garlic, just rub the roast with coarsely ground black pepper. Then serve the roast with a good prepared horseradish.

BASIC BEEF STIR-FRY

Learning to stir-fry can be intimidating, but ultimately it's very rewarding. This style of cooking opens all-new avenues for quick cooking. The ingredients need not be Chinese; for instance, stir-frying asparagus with garlic and olive oil is a wonderful method for creating an otherwise Italian vegetable dish. No need for a stopwatch. Your eyes and nose will clue you when the vegetables have gone from raw to crisp-tender, and when the meat, chicken, or fish is cooked just right. The ingredient list could have been shortened, but we wanted to balance simplicity, authenticity, and great taste. All of the ingredients are available in a well-stocked supermarket. Items such as hoisin sauce and oyster sauce will keep indefinitely in your refrigerator, ready for your next stir-fry. Serve this beef stir-fry with steamed white rice.

$3/4$ pound flank steak, trimmed of fat

Marinade

1 tablespoon soy sauce

1 teaspoon pale dry sherry

1 tablespoon cornstarch, mixed with 2 tablespoons water

1 tablespoon corn oil

5 tablespoons corn oil

2 slices fresh ginger root (about the size of a quarter), peeled and minced

1 small green bell pepper (about 4 ounces), seeded, deveined, and cut into narrow wedges

1 small red bell pepper (about 4 ounces), seeded, deveined, and cut into narrow wedges

4 scallions with green part, cut into 1-inch lengths

Sauce

2 teaspoons soy sauce

1 tablespoon oyster sauce

1 tablespoon hoisin sauce

1 teaspoon granulated sugar

1 tablespoon rice wine vinegar

$1/4$ teaspoon red pepper flakes (optional)

1 teaspoon Asian sesame oil

3 tablespoons water

1 tablespoon cornstarch

3 tablespoons water

Wrap flank steak in plastic wrap and place in the freezer for $\frac{1}{2}$ hour. (This will make the slicing process easier.) Remove plastic wrap and, with a sharp knife, cut steak across the grain into thin slices, about $\frac{1}{8}$ inch thick. Cut each slice into $1\frac{1}{2}$-inch lengths and set aside. Combine marinade ingredients in a medium bowl. Add sliced beef, cover, and refrigerate while you are preparing the other ingredients. (The beef can marinate up to 2 days prior to cooking.)

Prepare, measure, and mix the following ingredients in separate containers, as follows, and place them next to your stove before you start cooking. Place 5 tablespoons corn oil in a measuring cup. Combine ginger and bell peppers in a bowl. Place scallions in another small bowl. Combine sauce ingredients in a small bowl. Combine cornstarch and water in a jar with a tight-fitting lid. Remove marinated meat from refrigerator. Have a slotted spoon and a dinner plate right next to stove.

Heat a 14-inch wok or 12-inch frying pan over high heat until hot, about 1 minute. Add half the oil; when it just begins to smoke add beef. Stir-fry, using a spatula to separate the meat. When meat is nicely browned, 2 to 3 minutes, remove to reserved plate, using the slotted spoon. Return wok to burner, add remaining oil, and heat. When hot, add ginger mixture to wok and stir-fry until peppers are glistening and crisp-tender, 1 to 2 minutes. Add scallions and stir-fry 1 minute longer. Return beef to wok, including any juice on the plate, and stir to combine. Then add sauce to the pan and stir-fry until hot, about 1 minute. Push beef and vegetables to side of pan, shake the cornstarch-water mixture and add about half to the sauce. Stir to heat and watch how it thickens.

If lightly thickened, toss with beef and vegetables to coat; if still thin, add a bit more thickener. Remember, you can always thicken more, so go slowly with the cornstarch mixture. Toss 1 or 2 times to thoroughly combine, then remove to a heated serving bowl or plates. Serve immediately. *Serves 4.*

Cook's Notes

- All of your slicing and measuring can be completed as much as 1 day ahead. Tightly cover with plastic wrap and refrigerate. Remove ingredients $\frac{1}{2}$ hour before stir-frying.
- Use low-sodium soy sauce if you prefer.
- Oyster sauce is literally a sauce made from oysters; brown in color, it adds a fragrant flavor to Chinese dishes. Hoisin sauce is made from soybeans, garlic, vinegar, sugar, chilies, etc. Also brown in color, it has a pungent and delightful flavor. Oyster sauce typically comes in a bottle, while hoisin sauce is available either canned or in a glass jar. If canned, store remaining sauce in a glass or plastic container with a well-fitting lid.
- Red pepper flakes are found with the spices; store in the refrigerator to prevent flavor loss.
- Buy small quantities of fresh ginger at a time. It keeps well, if wrapped in paper towels and stored in the refrigerator, but after a while it will mold and should be discarded. In the market, it is OK to break off a small knob from a large root of ginger and buy just that piece.
- Other vegetables can be substituted for the bell peppers. Use asparagus or broccoli, for instance, cut into bite-size pieces. If using broccoli by all means use the stems; when cut

on the diagonal into "coins" broccoli stems are delightful stir-fried.

- ◆ If you are familiar with canned baby ears of corn, they can be fun to add to a stir-fry. Substitute for either the green or red peppers in this recipe. Drain and blot dry, then add along with the bell pepper to the stir-fry.
- ◆ If flank steak is not available, good substitutes are boneless strip steak, sirloin, or rib-eye steak.

STUFFED PORK CHOPS

These are fun to make and really don't require any special skill. You can cut the "pocket" in your own chops or ask a butcher to do it for you. The stuffing is seasoned with fresh rosemary and plenty of parsley, giving you a brighter flavor than many of the supermarket-variety prestuffed chops. You'll like them served with a rice pilaf, scalloped potatoes, or crusty loaf of bread and a simple green salad.

2 loin or rib pork chops, 1½ to 2 inches thick

2 tablespoons olive oil

2 medium-size fresh mushrooms, finely chopped

¼ cup peeled and finely chopped yellow onion

½ rib celery with leaves, finely chopped

1 tablespoon finely chopped fresh rosemary

¼ cup finely chopped parsley

Freshly ground black pepper, to taste

¼ cup unseasoned fine dry bread crumbs

2 wooden toothpicks or small bamboo skewers

¼ cup canned low-sodium chicken broth

1 teaspoon all-purpose flour

1 teaspoon Dijon-style mustard

2 tablespoons dry white wine or vermouth

Lay the chops on a cutting board with the meat, not the bone side, facing you. Insert a sharp paring or boning knife horizontally through the edge of the chop, pushing all the way to the bone. Keeping the opening as small as possible— 1 to 1½ inches—cut in both directions to open up a pocket in the meat without cutting through the edges facing you. Use your forefinger to help open up the pocket.

Choose a 9- to 12-inch frying pan (equipped with a lid). Heat olive oil over medium heat. Add mushrooms, onion, and celery. Sauté them, stirring occasionally, until vegetables are soft but not brown, about 5 minutes. Remove pan from heat and stir in rosemary, parsley, pepper, and bread crumbs.

When mixture is cool enough to handle, use a small spoon to insert stuffing into chops, using your finger to pack it in. When all stuffing has been packed evenly into chops, use toothpick or skewer to secure by inserting it at an angle across the opening through the top and into the bottom part of chop.

Rinse and dry pan. Place over medium-high heat until pan is hot, then add chops and brown on each side, 2 to 3 minutes per side. Reduce heat to low, add chicken broth, cover, and simmer slowly until chops are just barely pink next to the bone, about 25 minutes (add a few tablespoons water during cooking if liquid evapoates.) Remove chops to warmed plates and keep in a warm oven.

Bring the pan juices to a simmer over medium heat. Stir in flour, mustard, and wine. Cook, stirring to remove lumps, until juices have thickened into a gravy. Cook a couple of minutes to remove any raw flour taste, adding a little broth if gravy thickens too much. Pour over the chops and serve. Serves 2.

Cook's Notes

- **Try thyme or tarragon or basil in place of rosemary. And/or add ¼ cup whipping cream to the sauce.**

ROAST BONELESS LOIN OF PORK

Regularly available in nearly every supermarket or meat market in America, boneless pork loin is marvelously easy to prepare! Ideally, you will find a small roast that is not tied together with another in a butcher's netting bag like Siamese twins. A single roast carves easier and cooks a little faster. (The bagged version might take a little longer to roast and will yield two pieces of meat from each knife slice, but tastes just the same.) A little coat of pork fat on top of the meat is good, if you're so lucky, helping to keep the meat moist. Roast pork is wonderful served with some honey mustard, mashed potatoes, and a green or yellow vegetable.

1 boneless loin of pork (1¼ to 1½ pounds)
1 tablespoon olive oil
¼ teaspoon salt
Freshly ground black pepper, to taste

Preheat oven to 350°F. Dry meat with a paper towel and place it on a roasting rack in a baking pan. Rub meat all over with olive oil and sprinkle with salt and papper. Roast, uncovered, in middle level of oven, until pork registers 150°F when tested with an instant-read thermometer, 50 to 60 minutes.

Allow roast to rest, loosely covered with foil, 10 minutes before carving to set the juices and prevent juice loss on your carving board. Carve across the grain into oval slices about ¼ inch thick.
Serves 4.

Cook's Notes

- **Roasting is one of the simplest forms of cooking. A heated box (your oven) supplies dry heat that cooks and browns to some degree whatever you put in it. All you need do, once food is in your oven, is figure out when it is finished cooking. Experience helps and so does an instant-read thermometer. See the equipment section and buy one today if you don't already own one.**
- **Modern pork is bred to be lean and the loin is one of the leanest cuts. It will be dry if overcooked. Be forewarned.**
- **Boneless loin of pork is actually the center muscle from loin chops removed in a single long piece from the bones. The bones are then sold as pork back ribs.**

ROAST LEG OF LAMB

We suspect that many people who say they don't like lamb have never tasted it properly prepared. Lamb is one of our favorite meats. This leg of lamb—marinated with garlic and herbs—will convert anyone into a lamb lover. Most legs of lamb weigh no more than four or five pounds including the bone. Smile nicely at your butcher and ask him please to bone and tie it for you. Boned legs are much easier to slice and serve, and they cook in a shorter amount of time. Use the bone for stock or give it to your favorite canine.

1 leg of lamb (4 to 5 pounds), boned and tied
Salt and freshly ground black pepper, to taste

Marinade

Juice of 1/2 lemon
1 medium-size yellow onion, peeled and thinly sliced
4 cloves garlic, peeled and pressed
1/2 cup dry red wine
2 tablespoons olive oil
1/4 cup chopped fresh mint or 1 tablespoon dried mint
2 teaspoons dried oregano

1 tablespoon cornstarch mixed with 1 tablespoon water (optional)

Rub lamb with salt and pepper, covering all sides, and place in a shallow dish. In a medium bowl, mix together marinade ingredients, pour over lamb to coat well, and cover with plastic wrap. Refrigerate and marinate 4 to 5 hours or overnight, turning meat several times to mix well. Remove lamb; strain and reserve marinade. Dry lamb with paper towels.

Preheat oven to 425°F. Place lamb on a rack in a roasting pan. (The rack allows the fat to drain off during cooking.) Roast in oven for 15 minutes. Then turn down the oven to 350°F and roast, basting occasionally with reserved marinade, until the meat registers done when pierced with an instant-read thermometer. Internal temperature for rare lamb is 130°F; for medium 140°F; and well-done 150°F. Start testing for rare lamb after 35 minutes; well-done meat may take up to 1 1/2 hours. Allow meat to stand at room temperature 15 to 20 minutes before slicing.

The juices in the pan can be defatted and served with the meat. Use a gravy strainer or blot with paper towels to remove fat. Lamb drippings are not usually thickened, but if you wish a thick gravy, add a paste of cornstarch mixed with water to the drippings; stir and cook until thick, about 5 minutes.
Serves 8 to 10.

Cook's Notes

◆ **In the summer you can barbecue the lamb leg instead of roasting it in the oven. It is equally wonderful prepared this way.**

BRAISED LAMB SHANKS

Simple, warm, and comforting, this dish belongs in the realm of winter food when tummy and soul wish to be satisfied. Because the sauce for the shanks is not terribly thick, they are particularly good served with rice, or mashed potatoes, or something that will soak up a bit of the wonderful flavors.

4 lamb shanks (about 2½ pounds total)

3 tablespoons olive oil

Salt and freshly ground black pepper, to taste

1 large yellow onion (about 1 pound), peeled and coarsely chopped

2 cloves garlic, peeled and finely chopped

⅓ cup dry white wine

1 can (28 ounces) tomatoes, drained and crushed

1½ cups canned beef broth (or 2 bouillon cubes dissolved in 1½ cups hot water)

Leaves from 3 sprigs fresh thyme

Leaves from 1 large sprig fresh rosemary

Gremolata

Grated zest (about 1 tablespoon) of 1 medium orange

2 cloves garlic, peeled and finely chopped

½ cup finely chopped fresh parsley (preferably Italian flat-leaf)

Preheat oven to 350°F. Dry lamb shanks completely with paper towels. Heat 2 tablespoons of the olive oil in a 10-inch straight-sided frying pan with ovenproof handle over medium heat. (You may also use a flameproof casserole of similar size.) When oil is hot, add lamb shanks and brown on all sides. Remove from pan and season them well with salt and pepper.

Add the remaining 1 tablespoon oil to the pan and when hot add chopped onion and garlic. Sauté, stirring frequently, until onions are soft and just starting to brown, 5 or 6 minutes. Add white wine and bring to a boil. Return shanks to the pan. Add tomatoes, beef broth, thyme, and rosemary. Bring mixture to a simmer. Cover and place in oven. Braise until the meat feels tender when pierced with a fork, 1½ to 1¾ hours.

Toss ingredients for gremolata together in a small serving bowl. When the shanks are done, remove them from the braising pan and keep them warm. Place the braising pan on top of the stove over high heat and boil until the liquid is reduced by about half, about 7 to 10 minutes. Taste for seasoning and adjust with salt and pepper if necessary.

To serve, place a shank on each individual plate. Top with a healthy spoonful of sauce. Pass the gremolata for sprinkling over the lamb.

Serves 4.

Cook's Notes

◆ **This dish can be cooked 1 or 2 days in advance. This may even be preferable because it allows you to remove some fat that has congealed during refrigeration. However, when rewarming, remove the shanks from the pot and return**

< Braised Lamb Shanks

them only at the last minute before serving, so that they just get warm, but do not overcook.

- ◆ Braised meats sometimes separate from the bone after long cooking. If this appearance concerns you, secure the meat with a string before cooking.
- ◆ Gremolata is a sparkling blend of flavors used in Mediterranean cooking. It is not essential to the dish, but a very pleasant addition

GRILLED LAMB CHOPS

This is an anchor entrée on many fine restaurant menus around the country. The chops may be offered with Middle Eastern spices, or rubbed with garlic and olive oil, or encrusted with cracked pepper and coarse salt, or marinated in teriyaki sauce. However they are done, lamb chops grilled over coals or a gas grill yield some exceptionally fine eating. In this preparation, we use Dijon-style mustard, a marvelously versatile seasoning ingredient. When blended with olive oil and a fresh herb, it provides an appealing flavor addition to the richness of lamb. Try these with scalloped potatoes or a rice pilaf, and a green salad.

8 lamb loin or rib chops, 1½ inches thick

2 tablespoons Dijon-style mustard

1 tablespoon olive oil

1 tablespoon finely chopped fresh rosemary

Freshly ground black pepper, to taste

Prepare a charcoal fire (or light the gas grill) and spread the coals when they are covered in a white ash.

Use a chef's knife or boning knife to trim nearly all the visible fat from the edges of the chops (this will help control flare-ups on your grill) and place on a plate or platter large enough to hold them in a single layer. In a small bowl, mix mustard, olive oil, rosemary, and a few grinds pepper. Using a pastry brush, spread mustard mixture over both sides of chops.

Cook chops on a covered grill, turning once, until an instant-read thermometer registers 110°F to 120°F for medium-rare, about 5 minutes per side.
Serves 4.

Cook's Notes

- ◆ If you have no way to grill outdoors, try broiling the chops. Set them on a rack in a broiler pan to which you have added ½ inch water (this prevents dripping fat from smoking up your kitchen). Position the pan so the chops are 4 to 5 inches below the flame or broiler element and cook as above. Total cooking time is likely to be several minutes longer than on a grill.
- ◆ Vary the herb. Fresh or dried thyme or sage are good choices. Or, skip the mustard-herb mixture and just press a little very coarsely ground pepper into the chops, lightly salt, and grill.

BREADS AND SWEETS

Fresh from the oven to indulge the child in you—nutritious quick breads
and (mostly) decadent desserts

꿍꿍

WHOLE GRAIN NUT BREAD

This bread is slightly sweet with honey and filled with rich flavors of whole wheat and pecans. It is a fine breakfast or dessert bread, muffin-like in its texture but with plenty to chew on, thanks to the nuts. If you've never made a loaf of bread in your entire life, you may as well start with this one—it is that easy to do!

Nonstick cooking spray
1 cup all-purpose flour, plus more for dusting pan
1 cup whole wheat flour
$\frac{1}{2}$ cup rolled oats
$\frac{1}{4}$ teaspoon ground cinnamon
$\frac{1}{8}$ teaspoon ground nutmeg
2 teaspoons baking powder
1 teaspoon baking soda
$\frac{1}{2}$ teaspoon salt
1 cup pecans
2 large eggs
1 cup buttermilk
3 tablespoons unsalted butter, melted
$\frac{1}{2}$ cup honey

Preheat oven to 350°F with a rack in the center position. Spray the inside of a 5x9-inch loaf pan with nonstick spray, dust it with 3 or 4 tablespoons of flour, invert the pan, and knock out the excess flour.

< Whole Grain Nut Bread and Peanut Butter Cookies

In a medium bowl, combine both flours, oats, cinnamon, nutmeg, baking powder, baking soda, and salt. Stir thoroughly —use a large wire whisk if you have one—to make sure that the baking powder and baking soda are blended into the flour mixture well. Add pecans, mix again, and set aside.

Break eggs into a 4-quart or larger bowl and whisk together with buttermilk. Add melted butter and honey, and mix well. Add the flour mixture and, using an over and under "folding" motion, blend them into the liquids. Don't overdo this; it is better to see a few lumps than to have the mixture look like a milkshake with nuts.

Scrape the mixture into the prepared loaf pan and bake until a cake tester or skewer comes out clean and dry, 55 to 65 minutes. Cool 10 to 15 minutes, run a knife all around the loaf to loosen it from the pan, and invert on a wire rack to finish cooling.
Makes 1 loaf.

Cook's Notes

◆ **This is easily made in a medium or large food processor. Fit the processor with its metal blade. Place the flours, oats, cinnamon, nutmeg, baking powder, baking soda, and salt in the work bowl. Pulse the machine 10 times. Add pecans and pulse 5 more times. Empty the flour mixture into a bowl. Place eggs, buttermilk, butter, and honey in the processor work bowl. Run the machine 10 seconds. Spread the flour mixture evenly over the liquids and pulse a few times, just until most of the flour mixture has been blended into the liquids. Do not allow the processor to run steadily** for even a few seconds or a tough loaf will result. Scrape the batter into the prepared pan.

- **Use walnuts or almonds instead of pecans. Or add a tablespoon of finely grated orange zest.**

᭜᭜

LEMON BREAD

Sweet, tart, and sprightly, lemon quick bread is a great loaf for breakfast, brunch, or tea. It also makes a great gift wrapped in cellophane and a pretty bow. It is wonderful served sliced and toasted with cream cheese and jam.

1 stick (¼ pound) unsalted butter, at room temperature,
    plus more for pan
½ cup granulated sugar
2 large eggs
½ cup sour cream
¼ cup freshly squeezed lemon juice
Grated zest of 1 medium lemon
2 cups all-purpose flour
2 teaspoons baking powder
½ teaspoon salt

Preheat oven to 350°F. Butter a 9x5-inch loaf pan.

In a large bowl, using a wooden spoon, cream butter with sugar until fluffy or use the paddle attachment in an electric mixer. Add 2 eggs and mix until completely incorporated. Add sour cream, lemon juice, and zest, and again mix com-

pletely with the electric mixer or with the wooden spoon. Finally add flour, baking powder, and salt and mix very briefly with the electric mixer or by hand with a rubber spatula, just to incorporate the dry ingredients. Turn the batter into the prepared pan and smooth the top with a spatula.

Bake until a cake tester or toothpick inserted in center comes out clean, 55 minutes to 60 minutes. Cool in the pan for 20 minutes. Remove loaf from pan and place on a wire rack to cool completely.
Makes 1 loaf.

Cook's Notes

- **The bread is best baked at least a day before serving to allow flavors to mellow. It also can be done up to a month in advance and frozen successfully (well wrapped).**
- **This makes a fairly small loaf, but the recipe can easily be doubled to make 2 loaves.**
- **When adding the dry ingredients, be careful to mix only as much as needed. Overmixing at this stage could produce a tough product.**

᭜᭜

ZUCCHINI BREAD

This bread is so tasty, with its citrus flavors, that you may actually have to buy zucchini at the market instead of waiting for your garden to produce or for your friends and neighbors to give you some. This recipe makes two large loaves, one to eat now and one to freeze for another time—or to give to the friend who gave you the zucchini.

You can also make muffins instead of loaves or one loaf and a dozen muffins (see following variation).

2 small zucchini (about 8 ounces total)

3 large eggs

1 1/4 cups granulated sugar

1 cup vegetable oil, plus more for pan

3 cups all-purpose flour

1 teaspoon baking soda

1 teaspoon salt

1 tablespoon ground cinnamon

2 teaspoons grated orange zest

2 teaspoons grated lemon zest

1 tablespoon pure vanilla extract

1 cup chopped walnuts or other nuts (optional)

Preheat oven to 350°F. Wash zucchini, trim off stem ends, and coarsely grate—do not peel. Set aside. In a large bowl with an electric mixer, beat together eggs, sugar, and oil until well blended, 2 to 3 minutes.

In another bowl, mix flour, baking soda, salt, cinnamon, and orange and lemon zests. Add grated zucchini and stir to mix well and coat the zucchini. Add to egg mixture, stirring to blend, then stir in vanilla extract and nuts, if using.

Brush two 5x9-inch loaf pans with oil. Pour an equal amount of batter in each and bake until a cake tester or toothpick inserted in the center comes out clean, 35 to 45 minutes. Cool in pans on a rack for 10 minutes, then turn out onto a wire rack to cool completely.
Makes 2 loaves.

Zucchini Muffins

Pour batter into oiled cups of a muffin tin, about 3/4 full. Bake in a preheated 400°F oven for 20 to 25 minutes. Makes 24 muffins.

BRAN-BANANA MUFFINS

Bananas add taste and moisture to these delightful morning breads. Light on fats and easy to make, some can always be in the freezer for a quick reheat. In this recipe, make sure you use well-ripened bananas—with lots of brown spots on the peel.

Nonstick cooking spray

1/2 stick (4 tablespoons) unsalted butter, at room temperature

1/2 cup firmly packed brown sugar

1 large egg

1 cup bran cereal (not bran flakes)

2 medium-size ripe bananas

1/3 cup buttermilk

3/4 cup raisins

3/4 cup coarsely chopped walnuts

1 1/3 cups all-purpose flour

1/2 teaspoon salt

1 teaspoon baking powder

1 teaspoon baking soda

1 teaspoon ground cinnamon

Preheat oven to 375°F. Spray a standard 12-cup muffin pan with nonstick spray. In a large bowl, using an electric mixer, cream together butter and brown sugar until fluffy. (An electric mixer is very useful for this task, but strong arms, very soft butter, and a bowl and wooden spoon will do just as well.) Add egg and blend well. Add bran cereal and mix completely. In a separate, shallow bowl, mash bananas and buttermilk together with a table fork until slightly chunky; do not purée. Add this to the bran mixture. Blend in raisins and walnuts and mix completely.

Sift together flour, salt, baking powder, baking soda, and cinnamon in a medium bowl. Add sifted flour mixture to the batter in large bowl and stir just until flour disappears. Do not overbeat. Divide the mixture among 12 muffin cups, filling each about ¾ full. Bake until muffins are puffed and brown and a cake tester or toothpick inserted in the center comes out clean. Allow muffins to cool 5 minutes before removing from pan.

These muffins are best while still warm; however, they will keep for 2 days at room temperature. If you wish to freeze the muffins, place them in a single layer in a zippered plastic freezer bag. These will keep up to a month, if they last that long.
Makes 12 muffins.

Cook's Notes

◆ **The trick to making great muffins is not to overmix when adding the flour. Blend only until you can no longer see any white, then stop.**

◆ **Instead of buttering, greasing, or spraying your muffin pan, another foolproof way to avoid having muffins stick is to use paper baking cups. Just place one paper cup inside each muffin cup and fill with batter as described in recipe. This also gives you the advantage of some pretty little muffins to give as gifts.**

◆ **When a recipe calls for "tightly packed" brown sugar, use a dry-style measuring cup and scoop out a rounded measure of brown sugar. Tap down lightly with the back of a spoon, adding a bit more sugar if necessary to make the sugar level with the top of the cup.**

❦❦

BUTTERMILK BISCUITS

Simple, easy, and delicious, biscuits are a true American favorite. The only secret for making great ones is to use a gentle hand both in mixing and in forming. Many Southern cookbooks will then advise you to remove biscuits from the oven and place them directly into a tea towel for about half an hour. We find them mighty good with or without this last piece of advice.

2 cups all-purpose flour, plus more for kneading

2 teaspoons baking powder

¼ teaspoon baking soda

¼ teaspoon salt

½ stick (4 tablespoons) very cold unsalted butter

⅔ cup buttermilk

Preheat oven to 450°F. Blend flour, baking powder, baking soda, and salt in a large mixing bowl. Cut butter into small pieces (about the size of a whole almond) and add to the bowl. Using your fingertips and working quickly, rub butter into the flour mixture until it is the texture of coarse meal. Slowly pour the buttermilk into the flour mixture, stirring briskly with a table fork. Continue mixing with the fork until all the moisture is incorporated into the flour.

Turn mixture out onto a clean, smooth counter surface sprinkled with about a tablespoon of flour and knead several times. Add a bit more flour if the dough is still tacky, but be careful not to overknead or the biscuits will be tough. Pat dough into a circle about a $1/2$ inch thick. Cut the biscuits with a 2-inch round cookie cutter and place on an ungreased baking sheet. Quickly reknead scraps and cut 1 or 2 more biscuits. Bake until nicely brown, 12 to 14 minutes. Either cool on a wire rack or in a tea towel as mentioned above. *Makes 10 to 12 biscuits.*

❦❦

PANCAKES AND WAFFLES

It is our hope that the present generation of children will grow up experiencing something better than boxed pancake mix. There is a difference! Real pancakes and waffles, with pure maple syrup, are just wonderful. Adding fresh berries to the batter, or sliced fruit on top, just adds to the pleasure. Sometimes, instead of having pancakes for Sunday breakfast, we have them for dinner. Why not? Finish a lazy Sunday with a supper of fresh grapefruit, pancakes, and bacon or sausage. Young ones love the idea and the cook has time to prepare the meal before children are restless and starved!

2 cups all-purpose flour

1 tablespoon granulated sugar

1 teaspoon salt

$1^1/2$ tablespoons baking powder

3 extra-large eggs, at room temperature

$1^3/4$ cups milk (use only $1^1/2$ cups for waffles)

$3/4$ stick (6 tablespoons) unsalted butter, melted

Vegetable oil, for greasing cooking surface

Sift flour, sugar, salt, and baking powder into a large bowl and set aside. Separate eggs, putting yolks in a medium bowl and whites in another medium bowl. Add milk to the yolks, stir to combine thoroughly, then add to flour mixture. Stir just until the flour disappears—little lumps are OK. Now gently stir in the melted butter. Using a whisk, egg beaters, or electric mixer, beat egg whites until soft peaks form. With a rubber spatula, gently fold egg whites into pancake batter. Set batter aside to rest 15 minutes.

Pancakes

Place a heavy 12-inch frying pan (preferably cast iron) over low heat for 5 minutes. Preheating the pan is one of the tricks to making picture-perfect pancakes. Turn heat up to medium, brush in just enough oil to glaze the bottom of the pan, then ladle in the pancake batter. (About $1/2$ of a standard soup ladle or 1 large serving spoon of batter makes a 4-inch pancake.) Don't crowd the pan—it is hard to flip pancakes that have run together. When little holes form on top of the pancakes, lift up just a little of the side to check for browning; then, if nicely browned, flip the pancakes and cook the other side until nicely browned. (Do not flip your pancakes more than once—it toughens them.) Remove to a warmed plate.

To make a second batch, you normally do not need to add more oil, but if the pan seems dry, add some. Adjust the heat of your burner higher or lower depending on how the first batch came out.

Waffles
Preheat your waffle iron for 5 minutes. If your iron has a nonstick finish, then there is no need to oil the surface. Otherwise, use a brush or folded piece of paper towel to coat the surface lightly with oil. Add batter sparingly. If you add too much, it will ooze out all over the sides when you close the lid. Adjust the amounts according to the size of your waffle iron. Typically, when the "steaming" stops your waffle is done. Lift the top just a little to check. Practice will make perfect here.
Makes 25 four-inch pancakes or about 12 waffles.

Cook's Notes

- A griddle works best for making pancakes because it has no sides to get in the way of flipping the pancakes, but that is an extra piece of equipment for the beginning cook.
- Make your own pancake "mix" by premeasuring and mixing the dry ingredients. Place in a zippered plastic bag, label, and store. Now combining the mix with eggs, milk, and butter will be a snap.

- If you have forgotten to have eggs at room temperature, place the eggs, still in their shells, in a bowl of very warm water for 5 minutes or so.
- Substitute ½ cup whole wheat flour for ½ cup of all-purpose to make whole wheat pancakes.
- Add a sprinkling of fresh or partially frozen blueberries to the pancakes once you have ladled the batter onto the frying pan. Adding berries to the batter in the bowl tends to turn the batter blue, and the berries sink to the bottom of the bowl, which forces you to overmix the batter.
- Add 1 teaspoon grated lemon zest or ½ cup finely chopped pecans to the batter.

CHOCOLATE CAKE

For those of you who have forgotten—or never knew—how delicious and easy it is to make a cake from scratch, here is our offering. The recipe comes from a friend with a reputation for being an exceptional cook. It is a simple, not terribly rich cake. We like to bake it in square pans because it is easier to cut, but you can certainly use round pans or even an oblong one if that's what you prefer or have available.

Chocolate Syrup
½ cup unsweetened cocoa powder
½ cup granulated sugar
½ cup water

1 stick (¼ pound) unsalted butter, at room temperature

¾ cup granulated sugar

2 extra-large eggs

2 teaspoons pure vanilla extract

2 cups all-purpose flour

1 teaspoon baking soda

1 cup buttermilk

Chocolate Frosting, following

Combine ingredients for chocolate syrup in a 1½-quart saucepan and cook over low heat, stirring constantly, until smooth, 3 to 4 minutes. Remove from heat and let cool to room temperature (this will take about 45 minutes).

Preheat oven to 350°F. Line the bottoms of two 8-inch square baking pans with squares of parchment or waxed paper.

In a large bowl using an electric mixer, cream butter until it turns pale yellow, about 5 minutes. Add the ¾ cup sugar and continue beating another 5 minutes. Then add eggs, 1 at a time, beating until they are completely blended in. Mix in vanilla extract.

In a medium bowl using a fork, mix together flour and baking soda. Beat about ½ cup of the flour mixture into the creamed butter; then add ¼ cup of the buttermilk. Continue adding flour and buttermilk alternately ending with flour and beating after each addition. With a spoon, stir in cooled chocolate syrup and continue stirring until it is well incorporated and there are no white spots left in the batter.

Divide the batter equally between the prepared pans. Bang the pans once or twice on the counter to remove any air bubbles. Bake until a cake tester or toothpick inserted in the center of the cakes comes out clean, about 30 minutes. Place pans on a wire rack to cool for about 5 minutes. Then remove cakes from pans, peel off the paper bottom, and cool completely on the rack while preparing frosting.

When cake has cooled, place 1 layer upside down on a serving plate and, using a spatula, spread frosting on top of it; then place the other layer over it right side up. Frost the sides all the way around to cover and finally frost the top with the remaining frosting. You can make a simple decoration on the top by using the back of a spoon to make little peaks. *Makes two 8-inch layers or one 9x13-inch cake.*

Chocolate Frosting

¾ stick (6 tablespoons) unsalted butter, at room temperature

1 large egg

½ cup unsweetened cocoa powder

2 cups powdered sugar

1 teaspoon pure vanilla extract

In a medium bowl using an electric mixer, beat butter until it is pale yellow and fluffy, about 5 minutes. Add egg and continue beating a few more minutes. On low speed, beat in cocoa, then powdered sugar, a little at a time. Add vanilla extract and beat on high speed until the frosting is fluffy, about 5 minutes.

Cook's Notes

- In order to divide the batter equally in the pans, so that you have even-sized layers, use a kitchen scale. Weigh each pan with batter to be sure the amount is equal. You can also use a 4-cup measuring cup and pour an equal amount of batter into each pan.
- Instead of using square baking pans, bake cake in two 9-inch round cake pans or one 9x13-inch baking pan.
- Top frosting with chopped walnuts, pecans, or any nuts you like.

❦❦

STRAWBERRY SHORTCAKE

"As American as Mom and strawberry shortcake"? Well, the saying could go this way, as strawberry shortcake may be every bit as popular a dessert as apple pie. There are two schools of thought when it comes to shortcake. One holds that sponge cake is the true basis for shortcake, but we come down on the other side—the side that feels there is nothing better for shortcake than a slightly sweet, rich, crisp biscuit. Please don't plan your shortcake desserts solely around strawberries—raspberries, blueberries, and peaches all make wonderful shortcakes.

2 pints fresh strawberries
$1/3$ cup strawberry preserves or other berry preserves

Biscuits

2 cups all-purpose flour, plus more for kneading
$1/4$ cup granulated sugar
1 tablespoon baking powder
$1/4$ teaspoon salt
$3/4$ stick (6 tablespoons) very cold butter
1 large egg
$1/2$ cup milk

1 cup cold whipping cream
1 tablespoon granulated or powdered sugar

With a sharp paring knife, remove the hulls from strawberries. Cut berries in half (or in quarters if they are large) and place them in a medium bowl. Warm strawberry preserves in a small saucepan or in the microwave until melted. Pour melted preserves over berries and sitr gently with a rubber spatula to blend. Preferably do this several hours in advance so the berries render a bit of juice. Cover and refrigerate the berries. Pull from the refrigerator about an hour before serving.

Preheat oven to 450°F. Mix together flour, sugar, baking powder, and salt in a large mixing bowl. Cut butter into small pieces (about the size of a whole almond) and drop into the bowl. Working quickly, blend butter into flour with your fingertips until it is the texture of coarse meal. In a small bowl, mix together egg and milk with a small fork. With the same fork blend the egg mixture into flour and stir until all the moisture is absorbed. Turn dough out onto a lightly floured work surface (a smooth, clean kitchen counter is fine). Pat the dough into a circle $1/2$ to $3/4$ inches thick. Cut the biscuits with a 3-inch round cookie cutter and place them on an ungreased baking sheet. Bake until nicely brown, 12 to 14 minutes.

Not long before serving, lightly whip cream with sugar in a medium bowl using an electric mixer. Whip until you just begin to see the marks of the beaters in the cream. To serve, split each hot biscuit in half, top with a generous tablespoonful of berries. Top with the other half of the biscuit, more berries, and then a large dollop of whipped cream (or as much as your conscience will allow). Serve immediately before biscuits get soggy.

Makes 8 shortcakes.

Plum Cobbler

These biscuits can be used to top any number of cobblers. For a plum cobbler, use 2 pounds of ripe plums. Cut each into eighths and place in a large mixing bowl. Toss with 1 tablespoon freshly squeezed lemon juice, 3 tablespoons brown sugar, 1 teaspoon ground cinnamon, and a pinch of salt. Place this mixture in a 2-quart baking dish. Top with the biscuits, overlapping a bit if neccessary. Bake in a preheated 375°F oven until the biscuits are brown and the plums are bubbly, about 30 minutes.

Serves 6.

Cook's Notes

◆ **The biscuits can be made and baked ahead of time. Reheat gently in a 200°F oven for 10 minutes. They may also be frozen, well wrappped, for a month. Bring to room temperature and then reheat as suggested above.**

☙☙

GOLDEN RAISIN BREAD PUDDING

It is wonderful that there is a return to delightful home-style desserts. They are so easy and comforting, but this one is also pretty enough to serve to company. Try to marinate your raisins at least a day in advance. If you can't find golden raisins, regular black ones work very well.

2 cup golden raisins

2 tablespoons brandy (Cognac, rum, or hot water may be substituted)

1 small loaf or half loaf day-old French or Italian bread
    (about 12 ounces)

3 tablespoons unsalted butter, at room temperature,
    plus more for baking pan

5 large eggs

3/4 cup granulated sugar

1 1/2 cups half-and-half

1 cup milk

Zest of 1 small lemon

1/2 teaspoon pure vanilla extract

Pinch salt

A day or 2 before serving toss the raisins with brandy in a medium bowl. Cover and store at room temperature.

Preheat oven to 350°F. Slice bread into 1/2-inch slices and spread 1 side with unsalted butter. Cut slices into large cubes. Butter bottom and sides of a 2-quart casserole or soufflé dish. Cover the bottom of the casserole with bread cubes and sprinkle about 1/3 of the marinated raisins over the bread. Toss in another layer of bread cubes and then more raisins, repeating until both are used up.

In a large bowl, mix together eggs and sugar. Add all the remaining ingredients and whisk until well blended. Pour egg mixture over bread. Bake until puffed and well browned, about 45 minutes. (An instant-read thermometer should register 180°F when done.) Remove from oven and allow to cool for 15 to 20 minutes before serving; do try to serve while still warm.

Serves 6.

❦❦

CHOCOLATE PUDDING

This recipe was truly fun to develop. It had been a long time since any of us had made chocolate pudding. After years of making complicated desserts, it was delightful to taste something that was rich and creamy, yet simple to make. This would make a wonderful dessert for a dinner party or for just your family.

4 ounces semisweet baking chocolate, chopped into small pieces
1/4 cup granulated sugar
1 cup milk
1 1/4 cups whipping cream
1/8 teaspoon salt
2 tablespoons cornstarch
1 teaspoon pure vanilla extract

In a heavy 2-quart saucepan, combine chocolate, sugar, milk, 1 cup of the whipping cream, and salt. Stir, using a whisk, and cook over medium heat until the chocolate is melted and sugar dissolved, about 10 minutes. Remove from heat, but leave heat on.

Combine cornstarch, the remaining 1/4 cup whipping cream, and vanilla in a glass measuring cup. Blend, using a spoon, until completely smooth. Slowly pour this mixture into the chocolate mixture, blend well, and return to the heat. Stir frequently until thickened and mixture heavily coats a spoon, about 3 minutes. (An instant-read thermometer should register 160°F. when done.) The pudding will thicken considerably once cold. Remove from heat and divide among 6 individual custard cups. Or spoon entire mixture into a single serving bowl. Cover and refrigerate at least 4 hours.

Serves 6.

Cook's Notes

- **For those with a microwave, this recipe is a breeze to make. Combine everything except the cornstarch mixture in a 4-cup glass measure and cook on high power for 4 minutes. Stir well, cook an additional 1 to 2 minutes. Combine the cornstarch mixture as directed above, add to the chocolate mixture and cook on high power 1 minute. Stir well, cook 1 to 2 minutes more on high power, until mixture is thickened. Proceed with directions above.**
- **Substitute 1 to 2 teaspoons of Grand Marnier liqueur for the vanilla in the recipe.**
- **This recipe can be made a day ahead.**

❦

BAKED APPLES

In the late summer and early fall when apples are at their best, we love to make baked apples. This dessert takes very little preparation, and the apples can bake while you are preparing and eating dinner. Whether made for just the family or served to friends, this dessert seems homey and satisfying. Use any good baking apple available, such as Gala, Pippin, Winesap, or Golden Delicious. We see the latter in the market year round and its texture and flavor are greatly enhanced in the baking process. Be sure the apples are firm to the touch, whatever variety you buy.

> 6 baking apples
> 1/4 cup dark or golden raisins
> 3 tablespoons unsalted butter
> 1/2 cup pure maple syrup
> 1/2 teaspoon ground cinnamon
> 1/4 teaspoon ground nutmeg
> 3 tablespoons whipping cream (optional)

Use a glass or ceramic ovenproof pan just large enough to hold the apples. Preheat oven to 375°F. Core apples with an apple corer or a vegetable peeler to make a straight, neatly cored-out section from the stem end to the blossom end. With the point of a paring knife make a shallow incision in the skin of each apple, completely around the diameter, about 1/3 of the way down. This technique allows the apple to expand, but not burst, while baking.

Distribute raisins down each hollowed core. In a small saucepan, melt butter over medium heat. Stir in maple syrup, cinnamon, and nutmeg. Pour an equal amount over each apple, using all of this mixture. Bake, uncovered, 30 minutes. Baste each apple with the pan juices, then continue baking until apples are tender when pierced with a fork, 20 to 25 minutes. Serve warm, pouring pan juices over each apple. If you like, 1/2 tablespoon of whipping cream poured over each apple makes a delightful addition.
Serves 6.

Cook's Notes

- **If you have never used golden raisins, try them. They have a lovely honey-sweet taste.**
- **Nutmeg can be purchased already ground, but it is much better to buy whole nutmeg and grind your own. An inexpensive nutmeg grater is available at cookware shops. Buy one that stores the nutmeg right with the grinder.**

❦

POACHED PEARS

This is one of our favorite fall and winter desserts. It is very simple, but the flavors of the brown sugar syrup laced with citrus, cinnamon, and vanilla make it elegant enough to serve to company. Any leftover syrup (if there is any) is wonderful over ice cream topped with chopped pecans.

Poached Pears >

6 Bosc or Comice pears (about 2 1/2 pounds)

1/2 cup water mixed with 1 tablespoon freshly squeezed lemon juice

Syrup

2 cups water

1 cup firmly packed brown sugar

1-inch piece cinnamon stick

3-inch piece vanilla bean, split lengthwise

1 teaspoon freshly squeezed lemon juice

1 strip lemon or orange peel

Topping suggestions

Whipped cream flavored with a tablespoon of the syrup, or

Vanilla ice cream, or

Frozen yogurt or lemon-flavored low-fat yogurt

Peel pears, cut in half lengthwise, and remove cores. Place pear halves in a dish in a single layer and sprinkle with the mixture of water and lemon juice to keep them from turning brown.

Combine syrup ingredients in a 2-quart saucepan and bring them to a boil. Reduce heat, simmer for 5 minutes, and strain into a 10-inch straight-sided pan.

Drain pear halves and place them, cut side down, in the syrup. Simmer, uncovered, for 8 minutes, turning them and cooking only until tender when pierced with a fork, about 4 more minutes. Do not overcook, or they will fall apart when you remove them. Remove pan from heat and allow pears to cool in the syrup. Serve cut side up, spooning about a table-spoon of syrup over pears before adding one of the suggested toppings.

Serves 6.

❦❦

PECAN BROWNIES

Brownies are one of the easiest desserts ever to make. If you have a saucepan and a few minutes, you are in business. They are everybody's favorite. Dress them up for a fancy dinner with a bit of ice cream and chocolate sauce, or give as gifts wrapped in cellophane and tied with a pretty bow.

2 sticks (1/2 pound) unsalted butter

4 ounces unsweetened baking chocolate

2 cups granulated sugar

4 large eggs

2 tablespoons instant coffee powder

1 teaspoon pure vanilla extract

1 cup all-purpose flour

Pinch salt

1 cup large pecan pieces

Preheat oven to 350°F. Line the bottom and sides of a 9x13-inch baking pan with a sheet of aluminum foil.

In a heavy 2-quart saucepan, melt butter and chocolate over medium-low heat. Stir occasionally until smooth. Remove from heat for about 2 minutes and then stir in sugar. Stir in eggs, 1 at a time, mixing completely after each addition.

Add coffee powder and vanilla. Blend well. Add flour and salt, and then mix in pecan pieces.

With a rubber spatula, scrape the mixture into prepared baking pan and bake until cake tester or toothpick inserted in the center still has a bit of batter clinging to it, 30 to 35 minutes. (Brownie will be slightly undercooked—as we like it. If you like a dry brownie, cook slightly longer.)

Let brownies cool in the pan. When completely cool turn upside down onto a cookie sheet. Place a wire rack on top and turn over, allowing the brownie sheet to cool completely right side up before cutting.
Makes about 30 brownies.

Cook's Notes

◆　**These brownies actually cut best when well chilled or frozen. Well wrapped they will keep frozen for 2 months, thus making a great do-ahead dessert.**

◆　**Almost any nut may be substituted for the pecans. Walnuts and almonds are great; macadamia nuts are decadent.**

❦❦

CHOCOLATE GINGERBREAD

Try not to eat all of this at one sitting! It is wonderfully moist and spicy and full of the dark flavors of molasses and brown sugar. This gingerbread tastes terrific unadorned, but becomes positively illegal when topped with whipped cream sweetened with a liqueur such as Grand Marnier or Kahlua.

Nonstick cooking spray
1/4 cup all-purpose flour, for coating baking pan
1 1/2 cups strong coffee (see Cook's Note)
2 ounces unsweetened baking chocolate
1 stick (1/4 pound) unsalted butter
1 cup dark molasses
1 cup lightly packed dark brown sugar
2 large eggs, beaten
2 1/2 cups all-purpose flour
1 teaspoon baking soda
1 teaspoon baking powder
1/2 teaspoon salt
2 teaspoons ground ginger
1 1/2 teaspoons ground cinnamon

Preheat oven to 350°F, positioning rack 1/3 up from the bottom. Spray a 9x13-inch baking pan with nonstick spray. Shake the 1/4 cup flour all over the bottom and sides of pan, then turn pan over and rap it firmly on the counter to knock out excess flour.

In a 1 1/2- or 2-quart saucepan over medium-low heat, combine coffee, chocolate, and butter, stirring until chocolate and butter are melted. Remove pan from heat and stir in molasses, brown sugar, and eggs. Pour mixture into a large mixing bowl.

Sift the 2½ cups flour with the remaining ingredients into a medium bowl. With a large rubber spatula stir the flour mixture into the liquids, mixing only until most of the flour mixture has been absorbed by the liquid (overmixing toughens cakes). Use a whisk to break up lumps of flour. Pour into the prepared pan and bake until a cake tester or toothpick inserted in the center comes out clean, 30 to 35 minutes. Allow to cool for a few minutes before cutting into pieces.

Cook's Notes

- **This is a snap to make using a food processor. See the Whole Grain Nut Bread recipe (page 147) for the technique.**
- **Dark molasses and brown sugar have more flavor, but using a light variety of each is acceptable.**
- **Coffee used in baking may be freshly brewed or made using instant powder or granules stirred into hot water.**

❧❧

PEANUT BUTTER COOKIES

Recognized by the characteristic crosshatch from fork tines and by their peanutty aroma, these cookies are a never-ending favorite of all ages. They're great as is, or they can be dressed up with a spreading of chocolate frosting. The kids might want to add a few colored sprinkles on top of this as well for a party look.

1 stick (¼ pound) unsalted butter, at room temperature, plus more for baking sheets

½ cup granulated sugar

1 cup brown sugar

¾ cup chunky-style or smooth peanut butter

1 large egg

1 teaspoon pure vanilla extract

2 cups all-purpose flour

½ teaspoon baking soda

Pinch salt

Preheat oven to 350°F. With a paper towel, spread butter over 2 baking sheets or line with parchment paper. In a large mixing bowl using an electric mixer, cream the stick of butter with both sugars. Add peanut butter, egg, and vanilla. Mix well, again with the electric mixer. Add flour, baking soda, and salt, and mix just until all dry ingredients are combined.

Using your hands, roll the mixture into individual balls, about 1½ inches in diameter, and place 2 inches apart on the prepared baking sheets. With the tines of a fork dipped in flour, press down on cookie balls once in each direction to form a crisscross pattern. Bake cookies until firm and light brown, about 20 minutes. Remove to wire racks to cool completely.

Makes about 40 cookies.

Cook's Notes

- **We prefer to use chunky-style peanut butter for these cookies for the extra crunch, but they are great with creamy-style if this is what is in the fridge.**

INDEX

TABLE OF EQUIVALENTS

The exact equivalents in the following tables have been rounded for convenience.

US/UK

oz=ounce
lb=pound
in=inch
ft=foot
tbl=tablespoon
fl oz=fluid ounce
qt=quart

Metric

g=gram
kg=kilogram
mm=millimeter
cm=centimeter
ml=milliliter
l=liter

Weights

US/UK	Metric
1 oz	30 g
2 oz	60 g
3 oz	90 g
4 oz ($\frac{1}{4}$ lb)	125 g
5 oz ($\frac{1}{3}$ lb)	155 g
6 oz	185 g
7 oz	220 g
8 oz ($\frac{1}{2}$ lb)	250 g
10 oz	315 g
12 oz ($\frac{3}{4}$ lb)	375 g
14 oz	440 g
16 oz (1 lb)	500 g
$1\frac{1}{2}$ lb	750 g
2 lb	1 kg
3 lb	1.5 kg

Oven Temperatures

Fahrenheit	Celsius	Gas
250	120	$\frac{1}{2}$
275	140	1
300	50	2
325	160	3
350	180	4
375	190	5
400	200	6
425	220	7
450	230	8
475	240	9
500	260	10

Liquids

US	Metric	UK
2 tbl	30 ml	1 fl oz
$\frac{1}{4}$ cup	60 ml	2 fl oz
$\frac{1}{3}$ cup	80 ml	3 fl oz
$\frac{1}{2}$ cup	125 ml	4 fl oz
$\frac{2}{3}$ cup	160 ml	5 fl oz
$\frac{3}{4}$ cup	180 ml	6 fl oz
1 cup	250 ml	8 fl oz
$1\frac{1}{2}$ cups	375 ml	12 fl oz
2 cups	500 ml	16 fl oz
4 cups/1 qt	1 l	32 fl oz

Length Measures

$\frac{1}{8}$ in	3 mm	6 in	15 cm
$\frac{1}{4}$ in	6 mm	7 in	18 cm
$\frac{1}{2}$ in	12 mm	8 in	20 cm
1 in	2.5 cm	9 in	23 cm
2 in	5 cm	10 in	25 cm
3 in	7.5 cm	11 in	28 cm
4 in	10 cm	12 in/1 ft	30 cm
5 in	13 cm